JOHN STOTT

THE Birds

OUR TEACHERS
COLLECTOR'S EDITION

The colourful Chestnut-mandibled Toucan in the forests
of Costa Rica.

CANDLE
BOOKS

This edition copyright © 2007 Lion Hudson plc/Tim Dowley and Peter Wyart trading as Three's Company Text copyright © 1999 John Stott

Published in the UK in 2007 by Candle Books (a publishing imprint of Lion Hudson plc).

Distributed by Marston Book Services Ltd, PO Box 269, Abingdon, Oxon OX14 4YN

Worldwide co-edition organised and produced by Lion Hudson plc, Wilkinson House, Jordan Hill Road, Oxford OX2 8DR, England
Tel: +44 (0) 1865 302750
Fax: +44 (0) 1865 302757
Email: coed@lionhudson.com
www.lionhudson.com

ISBN 978 1 85985 635 2

Printed in China

Photograph acknowledgments
All photographs by John Stott, unless otherwise indicated.
All Souls, Langham Place: p. 81
The late A. P. Dowley: pp. 12 (bottom), 25, 33, 37, 47, 48, 49, 50, 60, 62, 63, 78
Tim Dowley: pp. 35, 72
Peter Wyart: pp. 8, 24, 36, 41
Natural History Photographic Agency: pp. 51, 57, 77, 78-79 (overall)

DVD authored and created by Matt O'Neill for ICC Media group. Copyright © 2007 John Stott. Produced and manufactured by ICC Duplication. www.iccduplication.co.uk

Opposite: The author observing a colony of Rockhopper Penguins on the Falkland Islands, which Latin Americans call 'Islas Malvinas'.

THE Birds

OUR TEACHERS
COLLECTOR'S EDITION

ESSAYS IN ORNI-THEOLOGY

JOHN STOTT

WITH PHOTOGRAPHS BY THE AUTHOR

'Look at the birds of the air.'
(Words of Jesus in the Sermon on the Mount, Matthew
6:26)

'You see, he is making the birds our school-masters and teachers . . .
In other words, we have as many teachers and preachers as there are
little birds in the air.'
(Martin Luther in his commentary on the Sermon on the
Mount, 1521)

'What it is to be man . . . oh, that we might learn this . . . from
the lilies and the birds . . . So in accordance with the directions
of the Gospel let us consider seriously the lilies and the birds as
teachers   . . . and imitate them.'
(Søren Kierkegaard in a 'godly discourse' entitled 'The Lilies
of the Field and the Birds of the Air,' 1849)

God our Maker . . . *'teaches more to us than to the beasts of the*
earth, and makes us wiser than the birds of the air.'
(Elihu in Job 35:11)

Right: A flock of
White Pelicans at Lake
Nakuru, Kenya.

Contents

INTRODUCTION

It is largely to my father that I owe my commitment to bird-watching. He was a physician (a cardiologist, to be precise), and like most scientists, although we lived in the heart of London, he took a lively interest in all branches of natural history. In particular, he was a good amateur botanist. So during the summer holidays, beginning when I was a boy of only five or six years old, he used to take me out for walks in the countryside, telling me to shut my mouth and open my eyes and ears. It was excellent training in observation. I was soon hooked.

When in 1945 I was ordained into the pastoral ministry of the Church of England, I returned to London and was surprised to discover that bird-watching was possible even there. Winter-visiting duck patronized the reservoirs, which supply Londoners with their water, and the Royal Parks harbour many species in both summer and

Below: The author admiring a Swinhoe's Storm Petrel on Chil Bal Island, Korea.

Above: All Souls Church, Langham Place, next door to Broadcasting House, the headquarters of the BBC in London.

winter. In addition, London's bombed buildings provided birds with excellent feeding and nesting sites. Kestrels hunted for mice in the war-torn ruins and reared their young on the ledges of precipitous walls. Black Redstarts availed themselves of convenient holes in which to nest, and, while I was serving Holy Communion early on Sunday mornings in All Souls Church, and there was no roar of traffic, I could distinctly hear the Black Redstart's rasping song while it perched on the top of Broadcasting House next door, the headquarters of the BBC.

Ten years later I began to travel overseas, to lecture and to preach, and of course I took my binoculars with me, for there are birds everywhere. The widely accepted estimate is that there are about 9,000 different species in the world. They occur in every zone and every terrain, from arid desert to tropical rain forest, in town and country, and from the Arctic to the Antarctic. Moreover, the variety of birds — in size and shape, plumage and diet, habits and habitat — is truly astonishing. Take size and weight as an example. The tiniest bird is the Bee Hummingbird, which is endemic to Cuba. From the tip of its beak to the tip of its tail it is 2.25 inches long, and without beak or tail only 1 inch. When it flies, it is easily mistaken for an insect. In fact, I have myself watched a Tody in the Caribbean chasing a diminutive hummingbird under the illusion that it was an insect, and suddenly giving up the chase when it realised that its prey was a bird not a bee! The Bee Hummingbird weighs 0.056 ounces, whereas a flightless ostrich can weigh up to 200 kg (30 stones). The largest flying bird in the world is the Wandering Albatross; its wingspan averages about twelve feet.

Roger Tory Peterson, who in his prime was the leading American birdwatcher, and who died in 1996, claimed after a long life-time of observing that he had seen about 4,500 species, just over half. Peter Winter, however, in his book *The Adventures of a Birdwatcher*,[1] describes his nearly 100 expeditions, which took him to all six continents and led to sightings of 7,208 species. But the record was held by Ms. Phoebe Snetsinger whose tally, when she died in 1999, was more than 8,000. For myself, although I have had the privilege of travelling in many countries and habitats, I have seen only about 2,500 species.

Right: An osprey perches on a lamp in Western Australia. Because it is a fish-eater, and because there are fish everywhere, ospreys are found on every continent.

At all events, only one person has seen them all, and that of course is God himself, their creator. '"Let birds fly above the earth", he commanded, "across the expanse of the sky." So God created . . . every winged bird according to its kind. And God saw that it was good' (Genesis 1:20, 21). In consequence, he is able to claim: 'I know all the birds of the air, and the creatures of the field are mine' (Psalm 50:11, literally). More than that, since Jesus said that not a single sparrow falls to the ground without the knowledge of God (Matthew 10:29; Luke 12:6, 7), he must know not only every species of bird but every individual member of each species as well. And that would mean many thousands of millions.

It was Jesus Christ himself in the Sermon on the Mount who told us to be birdwatchers! 'Behold the fowls of the air' is how the King James' Version renders his command (Matthew 6:26). Translated into basic English, however, his instruction becomes 'watch birds!' So we have the highest possible authority for this activity. Moreover, he meant more than that we should notice them. For the Greek verb employed here means to fix the eyes on or take a good look at. This will certainly include our study and appreciation of their plumage and behaviour. But the Bible tells us that birds have lessons to teach us as well.

As a matter of fact, Scripture bids us go beyond birds and include in our interest everything God has made: 'Great are the works of

Above: Martin Luther became quite lyrical when commenting on Jesus' teaching about the birds.

the Lord, studied by all who delight in them' (Psalm 111:2 NRSV). Since 'the works of the Lord' refer to his works of both creation and redemption, it seems to me that nature study and Bible study should go together. Many Christians have a good doctrine of redemption, but need a better doctrine of creation. We ought to pursue at least one aspect of natural history.

So over the years I have been trying to develop a new branch of science, which a friend and I have jocularly called 'orni-theology', or the theology of birds. It is founded on an important biblical principle, namely that in the beginning God made man, male and female, in his own image, and gave us dominion over the earth and its creatures (Genesis 1:26-28). Because we alone among all God's creatures bear his image, we are radically different from animals, even though we share with them the same dependence on our Creator for our life. But as we are different, Scripture expects us to behave differently. At times, we are rebuked for behaving like animals (e.g. 'do not be like the horse or the mule,' Psalm 32:9). At other times Scripture chides us because animals do better by instinct than we do by choice (e.g. 'go to the ant, you sluggard, consider its ways and be wise!', Proverbs 6:6).

Martin Luther, in his fine exposition of the Sermon on the Mount, became quite lyrical when he commented on Jesus' teaching about the birds. He wrote:

> *You see, he is making the birds our schoolmasters and teachers. It is a great and abiding disgrace to us that in the Gospel a helpless sparrow should become a theologian and a preacher to the wisest of men. We have as many teachers and preachers as there are little birds in the air. Their living example is an embarrassment to us . . . Whenever you listen to a nightingale, therefore, you are listening to an excellent preacher . . . It is as if he were saying 'I prefer to be in the Lord's kitchen. He has made heaven and earth, and he himself is the cook and the host. Every day he feeds and nourishes innumerable little birds out of his hand.'[2]*

1. Privately printed in St. Louis, Missouri, 1996.
2. Martin Luther (1521), *The Sermon on the Mount*, translated by Jaroslav Pelikan, Vol. 21 of *Luther's Works* (Concordia, 1956), pages 197-198.

1. THE FEEDING OF RAVENS:
Faith

The first lesson that birds can teach us is faith, that is, to trust God in all things, to trust him for the supply of everything we need. We are not to worry, Jesus said, about food and drink to keep us alive. 'Look at the birds in the sky; they do not sow and reap and store in barns, yet your heavenly Father feeds them. Are you not worth more than the birds? . . . How little faith you have!' (Matthew 6:26, 30 REB).

Perhaps you know the doggerel (for one could hardly call it poetry) which records a conversation between a robin and a sparrow:

Below: An adult raven visits its nest to feed its young. Hooper's Point, near Marloes Sands, Pembrokeshire, West Wales.

Right: An Arctic Tern feeds its chick; Alrö Island, Denmark.

Said the robin to the sparrow,
   'I should really like to know
Why these anxious human beings
   Rush about and worry so.'

Said the sparrow to the robin,
   'Friend, I think that it must be
They have no heavenly Father
   Such as cares for you and me.'
               (E. Cheney)

Below: An English Robin at a bird box.

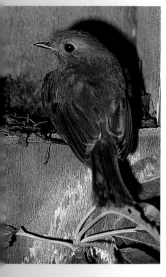

It is a delightful sentiment, although it is not a strictly accurate expression of Jesus' teaching. For he did not say that birds have a heavenly Father, but rather that we have, and that if the Creator cares for his creatures, how much more will our Father look after his children.

We must not misinterpret this teaching of Jesus about birds. There are three common misunderstandings.

First, Jesus was not prohibiting forethought. The familiar Authorised Version rendering 'Take no thought for the morrow' is seriously misleading. What he said was 'take no anxious thought' or

Above: The characteristic wise-looking head of a raven. This is Klaus, a tame raven kept at Wedellsborg, Denmark, in the 1960s.

Right: Yellow-headed Blackbirds nest colonially in North American reedbeds. This adult has a beakful of insects for its young.

(NIV) 'do not worry'. For of course we must take thought for the future. The Bible itself tells us to do so. The reason we are to imitate the behaviour of ants is that they store provisions in the summer (Prov. 6:6–8). Actually some birds do the same. Acorn Woodpeckers in California are adept at storing acorns in holes in trees or telephone poles, and Shrikes stock their larder by impaling insects on convenient thorns.

Paul's instruction to Timothy is germane to this: 'If anyone does not provide for his relatives, and especially for his immediate family, he has denied the faith and is worse than an unbeliever' (1 Timothy 5:8). Here is biblical warrant for a life assurance policy, or for an equivalent means of saving for the future. Jesus forbids worry, not prudence. Faith in God is not inconsistent with making sensible provision for the future.

Secondly, Jesus did not mean that God's children are guaranteed protection against all accidents. True, he said that not one sparrow can fall to the ground without our Father's knowledge (Matthew 10:29). But sparrows do fall to the ground, for example when chicks fall out of the nest, as Jesus knew perfectly well. Human beings also fall and injure themselves. And sometimes aeroplanes crash. What Jesus promised is not that the law of gravity will be suspended for our benefit, but rather that nothing can harm us without our heavenly Father's knowledge and permission.

Above: Puffins enjoy social gatherings when the sun begins to set. These birds are part of the colony on Skomer Island, off the Pembrokeshire coast, West Wales.

Below: The American Cardinal has a taste for corn on the cob.

Thirdly, Jesus did not mean that God's children can sit back and do nothing, leaving God to do it all. Even forgiveness and eternal life, which (because Christ died to secure them for us) are totally free and non-contributory gifts of God, still have to be gratefully received by us. And in every other sphere it is yet more evident that we have to co-operate with God, as the birds teach us.

For how does God feed the birds? The answer is that he doesn't! Or at least not directly. We must not imagine God feeding the birds, as we feed our pets at home, offering them food on our hand or on a plate. No, Jesus was an acute observer of nature. He knew that birds feed themselves. Some are insectivorous. Others eat berries, seeds or fruit. Some are flesh-eaters, others fish-eaters, while yet others are scavengers, predators or pirates. Some suck nectar from flowers; others find worms to their taste, and even snails! So what did Jesus mean? He meant that God feeds the birds *indirectly*. He provides the wherewithal for them to feed themselves. But they have to forage for their food. As the psalmist said to God, 'These all look to you to give them their food at the proper time. When you give it to them, they gather it up . . .' (Psalm 104:27, 28).

In a parallel passage in Luke's Gospel Jesus is recorded as having said not 'consider the birds' in general but 'consider the ravens' in particular (Luke 12:24). Ravens had already figured quite prominently in

What Birds Eat

Jesus knew perfectly well that different birds like different foods. Here are some examples.

Main picture: A European Bee-eater. What an exchange of rings is to human beings, an exchange of bees is to Bee-eaters. Mating takes place after the female has accepted the bee offered to her by the male.

Below: A Maribou Stork and a group of Vultures pick a carcass clean after the lions have feasted on their kill.

Above: Sunbirds have slender curved bills with which they probe flowering plants for nectar. This is a Scarlet-chested Sunbird, Kenya.

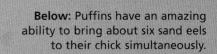

Below: Puffins have an amazing ability to bring about six sand eels to their chick simultaneously.

Above: Hudson Taylor, the pioneer missionary to inland China in the middle of the nineteenth century, was a notable man of faith.

the Old Testament narrative, in that a raven was the first creature to be released from the ark (Genesis 8:6, 7), and ravens were used by God to feed Elijah (1 Kings 17:1-6). Moreover it is twice said specifically that God provides food for ravens (Job 38:41; Psalm 147:9) – which indeed he does by making it available to them, for their diet is very varied. But still they have to collect it.

So faith in God is not incompatible with co-operation with God. We acknowledge that our food comes ultimately from God, and we rightly thank him for our daily bread. But we are still dependent on farmers and fishermen, and on the wholesale and retail trade. Again, when we are ill, we rightly pray to God to heal us. But if we are wise, we also consult our doctor and accept whatever treatment he recommends.

Hudson Taylor, the great missionary to inland China in the middle of the nineteenth century, who was also a notable man of faith, learned this lesson on his first voyage to China in 1853. He had promised his mother that in any storm he would wear a lifebelt. But when his boat was caught in a terrific tempest in the Irish Sea, and the captain of the sailing vessel instructed the passengers to put on their lifebelt, Hudson Taylor at first thought it would be lacking in faith to do so. Could he not trust God? But as he struggled over this question, he came to realise that faith is not incompatible with the use of means. 'The use of means ought not to lessen our faith in God,' he wrote, 'and our faith in God ought not to hinder our using whatever means he has given us for the accomplishment of his own purposes.'[1]

So then, this is the first lesson which birds teach us. Faith and works go together. Not indeed in salvation, which is by faith alone. But in everything else we both trust God and take appropriate action.

1. Marshall Broomhall, *The Man who Believed God* (China Inland Mission, 1929), p. 53.

2. THE MIGRATION OF STORKS:
Repentance

If birds can teach us faith, they can teach us repentance as well. For migratory birds, which fly away in the autumn, always return the following spring.

Now repentance and faith go together in biblical religion. The first recorded words of Jesus in his public ministry, after he had announced the arrival of the Kingdom of God, were: 'Repent, and believe the good news' (Mark 1:14,15). The same summons was faithfully echoed by his apostles. 'Repent and turn to God,' Peter cried in one of his earliest sermons (Acts 3:19), while Paul could sum up his ministry as a declaration to both Jews and Gentiles 'that they must turn to God in repentance and have faith in our Lord Jesus' (Acts 20:21). Indeed, the two cannot really be separated, since they are the two halves of

Below: A White Stork atop its huge and untidy-looking nest in Turkey.

Above: A White Stork's nest at Ribe, Denmark. This is about the most northerly limit of its breeding range; it winters in Africa.

Below: An Arctic Tern in flight, at Yellowknife, Canada.

the same action – turning away from idolatry and sin in repentance, and turning to God and Christ in faith (cf. 1 Thessalonians 1:9 and 1 Peter 2:25).

Moreover, what Jesus and his apostles called for had already been demanded by the Old Testament prophets. 'Return, O Israel, to the Lord your God,' pleaded Hosea (14:1). But it was Jeremiah who illustrated repentance in terms of bird migration. Here are the words which God gave him to speak in the seventh century BC. They may well be the first definite reference to bird migration in the literature of the world, although some two centuries earlier Homer in the *Iliad* had likened the retreating Trojan army to a flight of cranes heading south before winter.

> '*I have listened attentively,*
> *but they do not say what is right.*
> *No one repents of his wickedness,*
> *saying "What have I done?"*
> *Each pursues his own course like a horse charging into battle.*
> *Even the stork in the sky knows her appointed seasons,*
> *and the dove, the swift and the thrush*
> *observe the time of their migration.*
> *But my people do not know*
> *the requirements of the LORD.*'

(Jeremiah 8:6, 7)

Now Palestine was (and still is) a corridor of bird migration, popularly called a 'flyway'. Many species fly south in the autumn, through the Bosphorus, across Turkey and down through Palestine and the Nile valley, to winter in the warm climate of Africa. But when spring arrives, they all without fail return, first flying north, and then fanning out either west into Europe or east into Asia.

Jeremiah singled out storks. The Hebrew words translated 'dove', 'swift' and 'thrush' are less certain in their meaning. I have myself watched White Storks in springtime in Israel. In the early morning they feed in fields and dykes. But when the sun gets hot, thermal currents help them to lift off, and they soar to a considerable height of about 4,000 feet, before heading north to continue their journey. From their wintering grounds in southern Africa to their bulky rooftop nests in northern Europe they fly some 8,000 miles, their long red legs trailing behind them and their long necks stretched out in front of them.

It is reckoned that nearly half a million White Storks migrate over the Middle East every spring and autumn. They go and they return. The tragedy of the people of God was that they had gone away but had not returned.

All over the world the same mysterious North-South, South-North pattern of bird migration is repeated. The most extraordinary example is the Arctic Tern. Breeding in northern Alaska, Canada, Greenland, Lapland and Siberia, it winters as far south as the south-ernmost tips of South Africa and South America. Although it weighs only about four ounces, it yet flies from the Arctic to the Antarctic and back again every year, which makes a round trip of some 22,000 miles and is the most extensive migration of any bird.

Below: An Arctic Tern in its breeding territory in Iceland. It winters as far south as South Africa and Chile, a return journey of more than 20,000 miles every year.

Nearly as sensational is the American Golden Plover. Those whose nesting ground is in Alaska cross about 2,000 miles of open ocean non-stop to the Hawaiian islands, while some even fly on to Australia and New Zealand. Those which breed in the eastern Arctic, however, fly non-stop from Labrador to Patagonia, which is about 2,800 miles.

Above: A Manx Shearwater at the mouth of its burrow on Skomer Island, Pembrokeshire, West Wales.

Thus it is that birds 'observe the time of their migration', and do so with extraordinary regularity and precision. And what birds do by instinct (by inbuilt, inherited navigational skills which scientists have not yet fully fathomed), we human beings should do by deliberate choice, returning from our self-centred ways to the living God our Creator.

We should not imagine, however, that repentance is only an initial act which never needs to be repeated. For the sad truth is that we often stray from God in disobedience, so that we need to keep returning to him. To quote from Jeremiah 8 again:

> *Say to them, "This is what the LORD says:*
> *'When men fall down, do they not get up?*
> > *When a man turns away, does he not return?*
> *Why then have these people turned away?*
> > *Why does Jerusalem always turn away?*
> *They cling to deceit;*
> *they refuse to return.'"*
>
> (Jeremiah 8:4,5)

Here the prophet uses illustrations from human rather than avian behaviour. When we stumble and fall, he says, we do not wallow in the dirt or the mud; we get on our feet again immediately, clean ourselves up and resume our journey. Similarly, if we take a wrong turning, we do not persist in it; as soon as we realise we have gone astray, we turn round and retrace our steps.

The same principle applies to our walk with God. The people of Israel in Jeremiah's day were perverse and obstinate, 'incurable in their waywardness' (REB). We must not follow their bad example. Instead, if we fall, we must get up at once and go on. If we turn away from him, we must turn back to him at once. It is foolish to delay. We should not postpone our repentance or confession until our next Communion, or the following Sunday, or even our devotions that night. Wise Christians will not procrastinate, but repent, confess and seek restoration immediately. The penitential psalms (especially 51 and 130) will help us to express our contrition.

Above: A Grey (or Black-bellied) Plover lit by the midnight sun in the Canadian Arctic. Its winter range extends to all southern continents – Asia, Australia, Africa and Latin America.

Birds can challenge us here too, for in addition to their annual migration, many of them have a highly developed homing instinct. Even when they are taken to an unfamiliar place and released, they can still find their way home. Pigeons, for example, have been famous for this for centuries, indeed ever since Noah's dove found its way back to the ark (Genesis 8:8-12). During World War II 'pigeon post' became so valuable that the British Air Ministry initiated a register of carrier pigeons and sought to destroy all Peregrine Falcons, which are the principal predators of pigeons. In 1943 a special medal was awarded by the People's Dispensary for Sick Animals to a pigeon named 'Winkie', because it had helped rescue the crew of a Bristol Beaufort, which had crashed into the North Sea, by carrying an emergency message more than 120 miles.

Another example of the 'homing' instinct of birds is of special interest to me. Since 1954 I have had a cottage on the coast of Pembrokeshire in south-west Wales. Off shore are the islands of Skomer and Skokholm, on which more than 200,000 pairs of Manx Shearwaters (half the world's population) are believed to breed. Manx Shearwaters are birds of the open ocean, which winter as far south as the coast of Argentina. They come to land only to breed, and lay their single egg underground at the end of a rabbit burrow. In 1952 one was taken from Skokholm and released inland in Cambridge, about 240

Above: An Arctic Tern's nest, with eggs, at Sumburgh Head, Shetland, Scotland.

Right: A Manx Shearwater chick outside its burrow on Skokholm Island, off Pembrokeshire, West Wales.

miles away; it was back in its burrow seven hours later. On another occasion a Manx Shearwater was flown 3,000 miles from Skokholm across the Atlantic, and released at Boston's Logan International Airport. Twelve and a half days later it had returned to its burrow home, having travelled an average of 250 miles a day.

Would that we had as strong a homing instinct spiritually as birds have physically! The more we come to recognise that God is the true home of the human spirit, and that we are waifs and strays without him, the more quickly and painfully will we become aware of even the smallest estrangement from him, and the more eagerly will we return to him. For when we come back, we have come home.

3. THE HEAD OF OWLS:
Facing Both Ways

W hat is it about owls which inclines us to develop a love-hate relationship with them? They both fascinate and frighten us. On the one hand, their upright posture, fixed forward stare, ability to blink with their upper eye-lid, and facial discs like huge spectacles remind us of a rather pompous scholar and may be the origin of their 'wise old owl' reputation. On the other hand, they are mostly nocturnal, some of them have a penchant for cemeteries and ruins ('I am . . . like an owl among the ruins', Psalm 102:6), and they have an eerie repertoire of spine-chilling hoots and shrieks, so that in many cultures they are regarded as birds of evil omen.

Yet owls are superior to human beings in at least one important respect. I am not referring to their excellent eyesight, nor to their amazingly sensitive hearing, which enables them to locate a small

Right: A captive Eagle Owl in Denmark.

Above: John Bunyan, author of the seventeenth-century allegory *Pilgrim's Progress*. Characters in the book include Mr. Facing-Bothways.

rodent under leaves or snow, but rather to this: an owl's head is mounted on such flexible bearings that it can rotate at least 180° and even (in the case of the Long-eared Owl, it is claimed) 270°. So an owl's body can face one way, while its head is looking in the opposite direction. That is a gymnastic of which we humans are quite incapable.

Nevertheless, what we cannot do physically we can and should do spiritually. In John Bunyan's famous seventeenth-century allegory *Pilgrim's Progress*, the main character, Christian, who is on his way to the Celestial City, meets a number of interesting people. Their names tell us whose side they are on. Some of them are good guys like Faithful, Hopeful and Evangelist. Others, however, are evidently bad guys like Mr. Malice, Mr. Liar and Mr. Nogood. And one day Christian hears of a character called Mr. Facing-Bothways. He is a bad guy. He is neither a Christian nor a non-Christian. He sits on the fence. He tries to be what Jesus said we cannot be, namely the slave of two masters.

Yet in another sense every Christian should be owl-like or a Mr. Facing-Bothways, because all the time we should be looking back to the past with gratitude and on to the future with expectation. It is not easy to do both simultaneously. Some Christians are such avid futurists that they welcome only what is new and have no respect for the past, the old or the traditional. Others make the opposite mistake. They are such ardent traditionalists that they are resistant to all change. They are stuck in the mud, and the mud has set like concrete. Their favourite formula is 'as it was in the beginning, is now and ever shall be, world without end, Amen.' In contrast to these, according to the Preface to the Prayer Book, it has always been the church's wisdom 'to keep the mean between the two extremes, of too much stiffness in refusing, and of too much easiness in admitting any variation . . .'

Then there is another sense in which Christians are always facing both ways, for we are always looking back to the first coming of Christ on the original Christmas Day, when he came to the stable in great humility, and looking forward to his second coming at the end of the world, when he will come in power and great glory. Meanwhile, we are living in between times, between his two appearings, between kingdom come and kingdom coming, between kingdom

Above: A Barn Owl photographed at night in England.

inaugurated and kingdom consummated, between the 'already' and the 'not yet' of our salvation.

The Lord's Supper, or Holy Communion, constantly reminds us of these things for, as the apostle Paul wrote, 'Whenever you eat this bread and drink this cup, you proclaim the Lord's death until he comes' (1 Corinthians 11:26). It is truly remarkable that, within the compass of a single verse, Paul should refer both to the Lord's death (which is past) and to the Lord's coming (which is future), and should indicate that the Lord's Supper is a bridge between them. For when he comes in person, and the reality has arrived, the signs and symbols will no longer be needed.

So we must learn to imitate the owls, which swivel their heads right round. For then we can perform our essential spiritual contortion, looking back to Christ's death and resurrection with enormous gratitude, and looking on to his return with eager expectation. This is the only right way in which to be a Mr. (or Ms.) Facing-Bothways.

There are said to be about 140 owl species in the world. Most of my readers should have seen a Barn Owl, since its distribution is worldwide and its off-white plumage is distinctive. It can give one quite a shock as it floats by at dusk, ghostlike in its buoyant and silent flight. The Tawny Owl is also a familiar Eurasian species, which colonizes rural woodland and urban parkland, and which charms us with its haunting call 'to whit to woo'. Two more owls are quite commonly seen in Europe because they are both diurnal, namely the Little Owl and Short-eared Owl.

North America too is quite rich in owls. I have been fortunate enough to see the Barred Owl in Florida, the Spotted Owl in Oregon, the Burrowing Owl in California, and the Northern Hawk Owl in Alaska. Then once on the same day in Yosemite National Park I saw both a Great Grey Owl and a Pygmy Owl, which are respectively among America's largest and smallest owls.

But none of these is the owl I wanted most to see. I have had a life-long romantic fascination, which I cannot rationalize, for *Nyctea Scandiaca*, the Snowy Owl. The Inuit also feel its mystery, for it features in much of their mythology and art. They call it *ookpik*, although nobody is sure what this signifies. Richard Vaughan, however, in his

The Snowy Owl

Snowy Owls are circumpolar birds, which breed on the Arctic tundra in years when lemmings (their staple diet) are abundant.

These pictures were taken near Cambridge Bay in the Canadian Arctic.

Overall: The male Snowy Owl flies to the nest with a lemming in its beak.

Below inset: The female does all the incubating.

Above: A Snowy Owl chick hatching from its egg. The nest contained seven more eggs.

Left: The first chick to hatch is now a few days old.

Above: A back-lit shot of the Snowy Owl flying in to its nest.

Below: The male bird brings his mate a freshly killed lemming. There is a rapid transfer ceremony, then he flies off, while she feeds the lemming to her chicks.

Below (inset): The female at the nest site never relaxes her vigilance.

Above: The female Snowy Owl prepares to feed a lemming to her young.

Above: John and Mary, leaders of the Inuit community at Bathurst Inlet in the 1970s. They are wearing their Caribou-skin coats.

Below: A Gyr Falcon on its nest with its chicks on a cliff above the Burnside River.

book *In Search of Arctic Birds* (Poyser, 1992), writes that the Caribou Eskimos call it *ugpik* meaning 'wide open eyes' (p.24).

Let me tell you my story as it relates to the Snowy Owl. In 1971 some kind Canadian friends made it possible for me to visit Bathurst Inlet Lodge, some thirty miles north of the Arctic Circle. Originally a Hudson Bay trading post, it had been converted by Glenn Warner (a former RCMP) and his wife Trish into a summer lodge for wildlife enthusiasts. As Sunday approached, I asked Glenn if he would like me to arrange a worship service. 'By all means,' he replied, 'this community of Inuit are Anglicans, but they have not had a visit from a clergyman for more than a year. So, while you are about it,' he continued, 'they would like a baptism, a wedding and a Communion Service as well.' It was a moving service. Afterwards, in a jocular spirit, I said to Glenn that perhaps he should appoint me the Honorary Chaplain to Bathurst Inlet Lodge. 'Done!' he said, 'you are!'

So, in fulfilment of my chaplaincy duties, and thanks to the Warners' hospitality, you will understand that I was obliged to return to the Lodge on three further occasions in the 1970s! In addition to visiting the Inuit in their government-supplied, prefabricated, fibre-glass igloos, and officiating at services, there was still time for some bird-watching. Once the surface snow and ice melt, the Arctic wild flowers come out ('God's garden', I like to call it), and innumerable birds hastily set about the business of mating, egg-laying, incubating and parenting. For there is no time to lose before the first snowfall in August. A pair of Gyr Falcons had built their eyrie high up a precipitous cliff beside the Burnside River. And there were breeding Eider Ducks, Sandpipers, Lapland Longspurs, Snow Buntings, Golden Plover and other species.

Moreover, I do not forget the mammals: the Arctic Ground Squirrel ('*siksik*' to the Inuit because of its metallic chatter), the Barren Grounds Grisly Bear, Caribou, and the majestic Musk Ox, a prehistoric relic from the last Ice Age, which once roamed over much of Europe and Asia.

But where were the Snowy Owls? I had imagined that, because of their large size (they have a five-foot wingspan) and their brilliant whiteness, they would be very conspicuous. But they are a circum-

Right: The author on an all-terrain vehicle at Sachs Harbour on Banks Island in the Canadian Arctic. The driver is his friend, Steve Andrews, at that time Dean of the Anglican Cathedral in Prince Albert, Saskatchewan.

polar species, so that there are millions of square miles of the Frozen North in which they can escape detection, especially as some estimate that their global population may amount to fewer than several hundred birds.

Of course I had seen a pair of Snowy Owls in the London Zoo: the male being a poor old fellow forty-five years old with a double cataract! I had also seen Snowy Owls in private aviaries, and as winter visitors as far south as Chicago. One winter more than twenty were reported at Logan International Airport, Boston. For they soon grow accustomed to aircraft noise; there is an ample supply of rodents and rabbits for their diet; and human beings do not trespass onto airfields. But to see a Snowy Owl in an airport or aviary in winter is one thing; to see a breeding pair in the summer in the uninhabited Arctic tundra would have a romance of its own. So I determined to persevere.

In 1986 and 1991 I enjoyed two more expeditions with friends to the Canadian Arctic, reaching further north to Cambridge Bay, Frobisher Bay (now known as Iqaluit), Little Cornwallis Island, Resolute and Polar Bear Pass on Bathurst Island. We were enriched on these visits with sightings of Rock Ptarmigan, Brent Geese, Grey (in America 'Red') Phalaropes, King Eiders, Grey (or Black-bellied) Plovers, Sabine's Gulls, Tundra Swans, a pair of nesting Roughlegged Hawks, and three species of Skua or Jaeger (Arctic, Long-tailed and Pomarine), not to mention some pure white Arctic Hares and an elegant Arctic Wolf.

But still no Snowy Owls; only a brief glimpse of a single bird in flight perhaps half a mile away.

Above: Kevin Smart, Renewable Resources Development Officer at Cambridge Bay, holding a lemming.

In 1996, however, to celebrate my 75th birthday, I had the chance to return to Cambridge Bay. My friend Keith Todd was now in charge of St. George's Anglican Mission there. So, soon after his appointment, I had had the temerity to write to him and suggest that one of his first pastoral duties would be to find a breeding pair of Snowy Owls! He in his turn delegated this responsibility to Kevin Smart, who was the Renewable Resources Development Officer at Cambridge Bay and a keen amateur birdwatcher. Not long afterwards Kevin faxed me the good news that it was an excellent lemming year and that he had found a nest.

How can I capture in words the excitement of sitting in a hide, or blind, for hour after hour only a few yards from the bird of my dreams?! The 'nest' was no more than a scraping of bare earth, situated at the foot of a small protective rock and on a slight eminence. From here the sitting bird had a commanding view of the surrounding terrain and of any approaching danger. Because the Canadian Arctic is 'the land of the midnight sun', it was light enough to take photographs round the clock, including the early hours of the morning. It was a fantastic experience to eavesdrop on the domestic life of this majestic but elusive bird. She stared at me (although of course she could not see me), and I stared back. I could even watch mosquitoes crawling on her feathered face until she blinked and shook her head vigorously to dislodge them. One of her eight white eggs had hatched, and another followed two days later.

Every few hours the male would visit the nest with a freshly killed lemming. Then there would be a lemming transfer ceremony, as the female took the lemming from the male and fed it to her chicks. Next, he would fly off and she would return to yet more patient hours of incubating. Occasionally she would get up to turn her eggs, grunting as she did so, perhaps to imprint her voice on her chicks. And then she would lift her head to the sky and emit a plaintive high-pitched mew, probably to tell her mate that she was hungry.

It was the culmination of a twenty-five year search for a truly sensational bird. I felt I could now say my *Nunc Dimittis*: 'Lord, now lettest thou thy servant depart in peace . . . for my eyes have seen . . .' (Luke 2:29,30).

4. THE VALUE OF SPARROWS:
Self-esteem

O ne of the most crucial elements in human maturity is the development of a proper self-esteem. Some people have an inflated view of their own importance, while others have crippling inferiority feelings. In place of both extremes (having too high or too low a self-regard) we need to think of ourselves, the apostle Paul wrote, 'with sober judgment' (Romans 12:3). And in order to do this, we need to remember who we are, according to Scripture. On the one hand, we have dignity as human beings made in the image of God, and on the other depravity as sinners under the judgment of God. We are the products both of the creation and of the fall. This is the paradox of our humanness.

Of the two unbalanced extremes (superiority and inferiority), the second may well be the commoner today. Many people feel unwanted and unloved, and consider themselves to be worthless. So it

Below: *Passer domesticus*, the so-called 'English' House Sparrow, native to Europe, Africa and Asia, is to be found everywhere.

Above: A beautifully crafted Weaver Finch's nest from Thailand.

Below: A colony of Chestnut and Black Weaver Birds, on an oil palm tree at Ibadan, Nigeria. Some scholars think that the House Sparrow belongs to the Weaver family.

is exceedingly important that Jesus spoke of our 'value' as human beings, and compared and contrasted it with the value of sparrows. 'Don't be afraid,' he said; 'you are worth more than many sparrows' (Matthew 10:31; Luke 12:7). He deliberately chose the most insignificant little creature he could think of, and then argued from the lesser to the greater. If not a single sparrow 'is forgotten by God' (Luke 12:6), or 'will fall to the ground' apart from his knowledge and permission (Matthew 10:29), how much more will he remember and protect his human children?

This assurance grows when we recall that sparrows have a poor reputation and are often regarded as useless and disposable. To begin with, they may be the commonest and most widely distributed of all land birds. *Passer domesticus*, the so-called 'English' House Sparrow, is to be found everywhere. Native to Europe, Africa and Asia, it was introduced during the early part of the nineteenth century to Australia and New Zealand, and in 1850 to the United States in the hope that it would eradicate a plague of tree-stripping caterpillars. Some scholars place House Sparrows in a family of their own (*Passeridae*). Others regard them as belonging to the family of Weavers (*Ploceidae*), whereas the 'Sparrows' of the United States, such as the Song Sparrow, the Chipping Sparrow and the Swamp Sparrow, belong to the Buntings (*Emberizidae*). These two families together amount to nearly 700 species and constitute the largest of all bird groups.

Above: The unmistakable Victoria Tower of the Palace of Westminster, London. Sparrows have been cheeky enough to nest here and on Nelson's Column in Trafalgar Square.

The universality of House Sparrows is due mainly to their adaptability. They eat anything, and they nest everywhere. As for their diet, although they are mainly seed-eaters, they will in fact consume everything edible. As for their nesting sites, any hole or niche will do. In my home city of London they have been cheeky enough to nest 165 feet high on Nelson's Column in Trafalgar Square, on the Victoria Tower of the Houses of Parliament, in the right arm of the Duke of Wellington's statue (entry through a hole in one of his fingers), and even in the mouth of one of Trafalgar Square's bronze lions.

In addition to the apparent insignificance of sparrows, owing to their sheer numbers, some writers have spoken evil of their character. They are said to be cocky, noisy, aggressive, garrulous, impudent, peevish, and other horrid things besides. Buffon, the eighteenth-century French naturalist, wrote about the sparrow in very derogatory terms: 'It is extremely destructive, its plumage is entirely useless, its flesh is indifferent food, its notes are grating to the ear, and its familiarity and petulance are disgusting.'

Even Viscount Grey of Fallodon, British foreign secretary 1905-16, whose book *The Charm of Birds* (1927) has delighted generations of birdwatchers, could not at first find a good word for sparrows. 'Sparrows will chirp in the early morning,' he wrote, 'in such a manner as to be a nuisance, while other birds are singing. . . Their nests are so untidy as to be eyesores. . . They multiply exceedingly and damage crops of grain; they despoil crocus flowers.' What then is there to be said in a sparrow's favour? Only this: 'it is a bird; and being a bird it has feathers, and having feathers it has not been able to avoid a certain degree of beauty. . . Then it must be admitted that sparrows are very clever birds . . .'[1]

These largely negative assessments of sparrows make Jesus' positive reference to them all the more striking. For these little creatures, lacking both colourful plumage and musical song, are nevertheless cherished, remembered and protected by God, he said.

The so-called *Infancy Gospel of Thomas* [2] preserves a rather charming story (though almost certainly not authentic) of Jesus as a boy of five. He and other children were playing together beside a stream, and Jesus fashioned twelve sparrows out of soft clay. When his father Joseph asked him why he was breaking the law on the Sabbath day, 'Jesus clapped his hands together and cried out to the sparrows and said to them "Go!", and the sparrows took their flight and went away chirping.'

In contrast to this apocryphal story, what Jesus is recorded in the canonical Gospels of Matthew and Luke as having said about sparrows is certainly authentic. According to Matthew he asked whether two sparrows were not sold for a penny (Matthew 10:29). According to Luke his question was whether five sparrows were not sold for two pennies (Luke 12:6). This arithmetic has always puzzled commentators. But Adolf Deissmann in his famous book *Light from the Ancient East* (1927) offered a ready threefold explanation. First, of all birds sold in the market as food for the poor, sparrows were the cheapest. Secondly, they were sold either by the pair or in fives. Thirdly, the market price in the time of Jesus was a penny a pair, and, as a reduction for quantity, two pennies for five.' Here is Deissmann's conclusion: 'Poor, miserable little creatures, fluttering there, such numbers of them, in the vendors' cages! A great many can be had for a very small sum, so trifling is their value. And yet each one of them was loved by the Heavenly Father. How much more will God care for man, whose soul is worth more than the whole world!'

Mrs. Clare Kipps has described in her little book entitled *Sold for*

Right: Caged sparrows for sale in Jerusalem, in 1967, soon after the June War. Jesus asked whether two sparrows were not sold for a penny (Matthew 10:29).

Above: A cock House Sparrow on lichen-covered rock.

a Farthing (Frederick Muller, 1953) the remarkable relationship which she established during World War II with a little foundling cock sparrow, whom she called Clarence. Clarence had extraordinary gifts as both an actor and a musician, and developed an entirely uncharacteristic capacity for song. When he was approaching death at the age of twelve, Clare Kipps wrote: 'We are assured on the Highest Authority, and in no uncertain language, that no sparrow falls without the knowledge of the Father of Love. I have confidence that mine will not be an exception.' And so it proved. Clarence died on 23 August 1952, four months after the book had been finished. He was 'courageous, intelligent and apparently conscious to the end. The cause of death was extreme old age.'

It was in 1967, when she was an athletic teenager, that Joni Eareckson Tada broke her neck in a diving accident in Chesapeake Bay. It left her totally and permanently paralysed. After twenty-five years in a wheelchair she began to have health problems and had to go back to bed. Hoping to cheer her up, her husband Ken hung a bird feeder outside her window. At first she envied the birds their freedom. But then she remembered what Jesus had said about sparrows. She wrote:

Above: Joni Eareckson Tada.

'I glanced at the bird feeder and smiled. I could understand Jesus noticing an eagle. . . But a scrappy sparrow? They're a dime a dozen. Jesus said so himself. Yet from thousands of bird species the Lord chose the most insignificant, least-noticed, scruffiest bird of all. A pint-sized thing that even dedicated birdwatchers ignore. That thought alone calmed my fears. I felt significant and noticed . . . If the great God of heaven concerns himself with a ragtag little sparrow clinging to the bird feeder outside my window, he cares about you.'[3]

As Civilla D. Martin's old-fashioned American lyric puts it,

His eye is on the sparrow
And I know he watches me.

I return at the end of this chapter to where it began, namely the question of self-esteem. The only way to develop a true sense of self-worth is to come to recognise our value to God. Jesus declared on the one hand that not a single sparrow is forgotten by God, and on the other that we are worth more than many sparrows. It is an *a fortiori* or 'how much more' argument. If God cares for sparrows, which in some ways (as we have seen) are the most insignificant of all birds, how much more does he care about us? Indeed, he has proved his love for us in the cross of Christ. As Archbishop William Temple once put it, 'my worth is what I am worth to God, and that is a marvellous great deal, for Christ died for me.'[4]

1 Viscount Grey of Fallodon, *The Charm of Birds* (Hodder, 1927), pp. 232-3.
2 *Infancy Gospel of Thomas,* Greek Text A.II.1-4 [M. R. James, ed., *The Apocryphal New Testament*, (Clarendon Press, Oxford, 1924), p. 49]
3 Joni Eareckson Tada, *When is it Right to Die? Suicide, Euthanasia, Suffering and Mercy* (Zondervan, 1992), pp. 23-25, 178-9.
4 William Temple, *Citizen and Churchman* (Eyre and Spottiswoode, 1941), p. 74.

5. THE DRINKING OF PIGEONS:
Gratitude

It may come as a surprise to my readers to learn that birds can teach us gratitude. But it is so.

Gratitude is certainly a godly virtue, which should characterise all the people of God. True, during their wilderness wanderings, the Israelites were continually complaining against God and against Moses. Yet in the later liturgical worship of the temple one of the commonest refrains was 'O give thanks to the LORD, for he is good', with the congregational response 'for his love endures for ever' (see, for example, Psalm 136). Individual Israelites also learned to encourage themselves to give God praise and thanksgiving, indeed to thank him with all their being for all his benefits (Psalm 103:1,2).

If that was the case in Old Testament days, how much more should it be so for New Testament Christians! During his public ministry,

Below: A cockerel with upturned head, its characteristic drinking position. As the proverb says, *'Even the chicken, when it drinks, lifts its head to heaven to thank God for the water.'*

Above: A Native Pigeon, or Kereru, on Hen Island, New Zealand.

when Jesus healed ten men suffering from leprosy, he expressed astonishment that only one of them came back to give thanks (Luke 17:11-19). If we have even tasted the grace of God, gratitude should arise spontaneously within us. So when Paul prayed for his Colossian friends, he included the petition that they might be 'joyfully giving thanks to the Father' for their salvation (Colossians 1:11, 12) – yes and for other blessings too. In the 1662 Prayer Book the beautifully worded 'General Thanksgiving' expresses our gratitude to God 'for our creation, preservation, and all the blessings of this life', but above all for his 'inestimable love in the redemption of the world by our Lord Jesus Christ', and for both 'the means of grace' and 'the hope of glory'.

But what has all this to do with birds? Let me tell you. Come with me in your imagination to the country of Ghana on the coast of West Africa. Many Africans love proverbs and the pithy truths which they contain. But Ghanaians outshine their fellow West Africans in their devotion to proverbial wisdom. They seem to have a proverb for everything, and when I was there a few years ago, I began to make a collection of them. They have an excellent proverb on gratitude, and this is where birds come into the picture.

'Even the chicken, when it drinks,
lifts its head to heaven to thank God for the water.'

Behind this proverb lies the observation that not only chickens but all birds drink by gravity. That is, they dip their beak in the water, take and hold a sip of it, and then lift their heads high in the air until the water trickles down their throat. Of course they are not literally thanking God for the water, but they look as if they are, and Ghanaians have turned their action into a parable.

Did I say that 'all birds' drink in this way, by gravity? I did; but I was wrong. The class *aves* (birds) is divided into twenty-seven orders. And all of them practice trickle-down drinking except one, namely the order *Columbiformes*, to which the 250 or so pigeons and doves of the world belong. They drink by suction (like horses!), not by gravity. So they dip their beak in a pool or puddle and suck. They never 'lift

Above: London pigeons drinking from the fountains in Trafalgar Square, famous for its flocks of these birds. Pigeons drink by suction.

their head to heaven to thank God for the water'. In consequence, and in a jocular way, I sometimes refer to pigeons and doves as the most pagan birds in the world, since they are entirely wanting in gratitude!

In other ways, however, doves redeem their reputation. For they occupy an honourable place in the biblical story. It was a dove which announced the end of the Flood, by bringing Noah 'a freshly plucked olive leaf' (Genesis 8:11), so that he has been called 'the world's first pigeon fancier'. And it was 'like a dove' that the Holy Spirit descended on Jesus at his baptism (Mark 1:10). Thus, a dove was given a prominent place at the beginning of two new eras of grace, one following the Flood, and the other inaugurating the ministry of Jesus. If their drinking habits make them look ungrateful, we must remember that Jesus called them 'innocent', for he told his disciples to be 'as innocent as doves' (Matthew 10:16).

In North America there are only eight native and resident pigeons and doves. The most familiar is the Mourning Dove, so called because of its monotonous, lugubrious call. It is found all over the United States, and in every month of the year it is nesting somewhere.

Also very well-known is the common domestic pigeon, which populates most of the cities of the world. It is not a native North

Above: A White-winged Dove at Big Bend, Texas.

American bird, however, having been introduced. In fact it has been domesticated for thousands of years. It is descended from the wild Rock Dove of the sea cliffs. Accustomed to building its nest on a cliff ledge, it has no difficulty in adapting to the ledges of buildings. Breeding as it does in great numbers, it tends to be something of a nuisance. Back in 1385 the Bishop of London complained about the mess they were making on St. Paul's Cathedral. And Samuel Pepys, the famous English diarist, describes how, during the Fire of London in 1666, the pigeons were reluctant to leave their homes and so lingered until their wings were singed and they fell to their death.

It is always a delight to watch the courtship display of members of the pigeon family. A male will strut pompously round the female of his choice, now pirouetting, now bobbing and bowing, all the time exposing his iridescent green neck feathers and cooing most piteously. But next time you spot a pigeon or a dove, see if I'm not right in saying that it drinks by suction, without lifting its head to heaven, but keeping its beak in the puddle. And let its omission challenge us at least to lift our hearts (if not our heads) to God in thankfulness for his many and great mercies.

Saying grace before meals is an excellent habit, especially at home with the family. Then the children will learn early in life that it is a

Right: An endemic Galapagos Dove on Santa Fe Island.

good thing to acknowledge our humble dependence on God, and our gratitude for his provision of all our needs.

But we must not limit our thanksgiving to our food. We need to be thankful for all God's gifts. When the late Henri Nouwen visited Latin America, he entitled his published journal *Gracias*; and in his conclusion he explained why:

Above: A European Wood Pigeon photographed in St. James's Park, London.

> *Whatever is given — money, food, work, a handshake, a smile, a good word or an embrace — is a reason to rejoice and say* gracias. . . *I learned that everything that is, is freely given by the God of love. All is grace. Light and water, shelter and food, work and free time, children, parents and grandparents, birth and death — it is all given to us. Why? So that we can say* gracias, *thanks . . .*[1]

G. K. Chesterton expressed this very same truth with his customary vigour:

> *You say grace before meals.*
> *All right.*
> *But I say grace before the play and the opera,*
> *And grace before the concert and pantomime,*
> *And grace before I open a book,*
> *And grace before sketching, painting,*
> *Swimming, fencing, boxing, walking, playing, dancing;*
> *And grace before I dip the pen in the ink.*[2]

1 Henri Nouwen, *Gracias, a Latin American Journal* (1983, Orbis 1993), p. 187.
2 Quoted in Dudley Barker, *G. K. Chesterton, A Biography* (Constable, 1973), p.65, from unpublished notebook jottings.

Albatrosses

In popular legend, as developed in the English writer Coleridge's famous poem *The Ancient Mariner*, albatrosses are creatures of ill omen. But in reality they are magnificent birds of the open southern oceans. They can glide immense distances on their long, narrow wings, holding them almost motionless for hours on end. They come to land only to breed. Their elaborate courtship display includes bowing, dancing, bill clapping and preening, and the breeding cycle of the largest (the Wandering Albatross) lasts almost exactly a year.

Overall: A Black-browed Albatross in flight.

Above: A courting pair of Laysan Albatrosses, near Kilauea Point, Hawaii.

Below: A Black-browed Albatross wheeling over the South Atlantic.

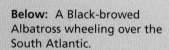

Right: A Waved Albatross with chick; Española Island, Galapagos.

44

Left: A Black-browed Albatross perched precariously on its cup-shaped nest, Keppel Island, Falklands.

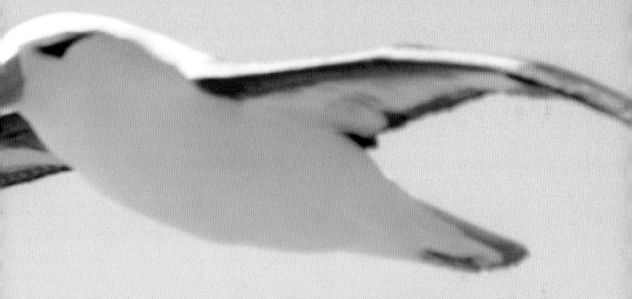

Below: Portrait of a Black-browed Albatross.

6. THE METABOLISM OF HUMMINGBIRDS:
Work

Above: A Swallow-tailed Hummingbird at a feeder, Niteroi, Brazil.

Have you ever puzzled over this agelong conundrum: do we eat to live or live to eat? In one sense there is truth in both, since life and food inevitably depend on each other. If we don't eat we won't survive, and if we don't survive we won't be able to eat.

The puzzle is more significant than it first sounds, for what is at stake is the very nature of our identity as human beings and the place of constructive work in our human life. The ability to work is one of our unique human qualities. To be sure, the animal creation is kept busy. Birds and beasts occupy their time hunting, eating, drinking, washing, playing. Yet these activities are not comparable to human work. As Pope John Paul II wrote in the introduction to his *Encyclical on Human Work* (*Laborem Exercens 1981*), 'work is one of the

Right: A Green Thorntail near Selva Verde, Costa Rica. Frenetic flight is more characteristic of hummingbirds than perching.

Above: A Rufous-breasted Hermit hovers at the opening to its nest.

characteristics that distinguish man from the rest of creatures whose activity for sustaining their lives cannot be called work.' For work is meaningful and purposive activity, undertaken with a special goal in view, whereas animals are not capable of understanding or developing 'meanings', 'purposes' or 'goals'. They cannot look beyond *what* they are doing to reflect on *why* they are doing it. They do not eat in order to work, but in order to survive. Their sole motivation is the instinct for survival.

I take as an example of activity which has no object beyond self-service and survival, the frenetic lifestyle of hummingbirds. Let me first tell you something about them. There are reckoned to be about 320 species of hummingbird, all of which are to be found in North, Central and South America, together with the Caribbean. There are no hummingbirds in Europe, Africa, Asia or Australasia. Their largest concentration is in the equatorial regions of Colombia, Venezuela, Ecuador and Brazil, and they occur in garden, desert, jungle and mountain habitats. Only twelve are native to North America, and of these only one is found east of the Mississippi River, namely the Rubythroat.

Most hummingbirds are very colourful, having iridescent green, blue, purple, red or yellow feathers on their gorget, crown, breast or

Above: A Copper-rumped Hummingbird.

tail. John James Audubon (1785-1851), the pioneer of American birdwatchers and bird artists, once described a hummingbird as 'a glittering fragment of the rainbow'. It is not surprising that many of their popular English names allude to jewels like topaz, sapphire, amethyst, ruby or lazuli.

The other well-known feature of hummingbirds, which is specially germane to this chapter, is their flight. They are capable of fantastic aerobatics, and can manoeuvre themselves more skilfully than a helicopter. For they can fly upwards and downwards, backwards as well as forwards, sideways and even upside down. They can also loop the loop and hover, holding their body motionless. Moreover the rapidity of their wing beat is phenomenal. The average is about twenty-five times a second, but in fast flight they can beat eighty times a second, and on headlong nuptial display (it is said) can even reach 200 times a second. At this rate they resemble insects, for the wing beat of the house fly (*Musca domestica*) is the same, whereas the wing stroke frequency of a mosquito varies 'from about 250 to 500 per second according to species'.[1] Although hummingbirds perch when resting or roosting, they hardly ever walk or hop. They move only by flight, and they feed, drink and bathe on the wing.

It is this enormous expenditure of energy which makes eating the dominant activity of their lives. Crawford H. Greenewalt tells us that he caught 'Hummingbird fever' in 1953. He developed an electronic flash of thirty-millionths of a second to 'freeze' hummingbirds in flight, travelled 100,000 miles in pursuit of them, and published his monograph *Hummingbirds*, illustrated by spectacular photographs, in 1960. Here is his conclusion about the metabolism of hummingbirds: 'Hummingbirds have the highest energy output per unit of weight of any living warm-blooded animal.' Whereas the average daily output of a 170-pound man is about 3,500 calories, the equivalent for a hummingbird would be about 155,000 calories. A normal man eats two to two-and-a-half pounds of food daily; but if his energy output were that of a hummingbird, he would have to eat 370 pounds of boiled potatoes a day. In fact, 'the average hummingbird consumes half its weight of sugar daily, an extraordinary intake.'[2]

And when a hummingbird's eggs hatch, and the young begin to

Right: A Ruby Topaz on its nest. All hummingbirds dart restlessly from flower to flower in order to replace lost energy.

grow, the mother bird has to increase her foraging in order to feed her brood as well as herself. Crawford Greenewalt catches the frenzy of this procedure: 'Feeding is an awesome spectacle. Probing deeply with her beak into the throats of the young, she pumps in a regurgitated formula in a series of convulsive thrusts' (p. 26). Indeed, 'she inserts her bill to a depth that makes one certain it will come through on the other side . . . The longer the bill, the more terrifying the process.' (p. 24).

Thus hummingbirds are almost continuously eating during the daytime, consuming an enormous quantity of nectar and (for protein) of minute insects and spiders. They hardly ever stop. Food gathering has become their chief occupation. They have to eat in order to replace lost energy, but they lose more energy in doing so, as they dart restlessly from flower to flower. They are caught in a vicious circle as through the process of eating they both acquire energy and expend it, and are then driven to replace what they have acquired and spent. Consumption has become the main business of their existence.

We human beings should differ radically from the frantic eating habits of hummingbirds, and that in two respects. First, we are not to become preoccupied with food. Jesus himself specifically told us not to be anxious about what we eat and drink, for that is the obsession of pagans (Matthew 6:31,32). At the same time, we are not to go

Above: A Green Hermit (Hummingbird).

to the opposite extreme and become ascetics, living an austere life which treats material things with contempt. No, God both created the material order and now 'richly provides us with everything for our enjoyment', if we can receive it with thanksgiving (1 Timothy 4:3-5; 6:17). So it is right to enjoy our food and to say grace over it. It is true that mealtimes vary from culture to culture, and that in famine conditions people feel blessed to receive even one meal a day. But when food is plentiful, most cultures enjoy three daily meals and transform them into rich social occasions.

The second difference between human beings and hummingbirds is that for us feeding is never an end in itself, but always the means to a higher end. We look beyond our eating to the work we are able to do because our bodies are healthy and strong. We eat in order to refuel. We do not eat in order to have energy to go on eating, but in order to have energy to do the work to which God has called us.

Let me quote again from the papal encyclical, *Laborem Exercens.* 'The church finds in the very first pages of the Book of Genesis the source of her conviction that work is a fundamental dimension of human existence on earth' (para. 13). 'Work is a good thing for man – a good thing for his humanity – because through work man not only transforms nature, adapting it to his own needs, but he also achieves fulfilment as a human being and indeed in a sense becomes "more a human being"'(para. 40). 'Man's life is built up every day from work, from work it derives its specific dignity' (para. 3). This dignity is the conscious privilege of co-operating with God in the transformation of nature.

1 J.D. Gillett: *The Mosquito* (Doubleday, 1972) p. 101.
2 Crawford H. Greenewalt: *Hummingbirds* (Doubleday, 1960), p. 9. See also Andrew Cleave: *Hummingbirds* (Hamlyn, 1989), which has even more magnificent photographs.

7. THE SOARING OF EAGLES:
Freedom

We human beings are by nature terrestrial, clodhopping creatures. The law of gravity keeps us earth-bound. So we look on the birds with envy. If only we could fly! We sigh longingly with the psalmist: 'Oh, that I had the wings of a dove! I would flee far away . . .' (Psalm 55:8). Flight is to us the symbol of freedom.

So throughout history the dream of human flight has persisted. It was first expressed in the Greek myth of Daedalus, the architect and sculptor who, in order to escape from his incarceration on the island of Crete, designed wings for himself and his son Icarus, which were fashioned out of feathers and wax. But Icarus ignored his father's warning and flew too close to the sun, so that the wax melted and he fell to his death in the Aegean Sea. In the sixteenth century Leonardo da Vinci became obsessed with the dream, studied closely the anatomy

Right: A Bald Eagle, near Mount Silkin, Alaska, USA. On 20 June 1782 Congress voted to adopt the Bald Eagle as the national symbol of America.

Above: James Cook, the English explorer. As he returned home in *Resolution* in 1774, after circumnavigating the South Pole, an Albatross joined the ship.

Above: One of the finest flying seabirds is the Redbilled Tropicbird, pictured here on Daphne Island, Galapagos.

and physiology of birds, and left behind him his 'Codex on the Flight of Birds', full of bird sketches and of drawings related to the possibility of human flight. Yet not until 1903 did those American aviation pioneers, the Wright brothers, succeed in flying the first powered plane.

How clumsy, however, are our most sophisticated aircraft in comparison to the simplicity and versatility of bird flight! Birds can climb, soar, glide, flap, hover, roll and dive. Their flight is possible only because of a fantastic combination of their light skeleton of hollow bones, their strong breast muscles, their stream-lined body, and their flexible wings whose every feather can operate independently.

Observers have constantly marvelled at the achievements of flying birds. Consider the distance, height, speed, tenacity and nobility of their flight. For distance we take the European Swift as our example. Since it is thought to fly an average of 500 miles every day, in search of insects, and since it migrates annually to South Africa and back, it must during its lifetime cover about three million miles. As for height, Barheaded Geese annually cross the Himalayas from their Central Asian breeding territory to their winter quarters in India, and a Rüppell's Griffon Vulture was once hit by a plane in West Africa at 37,000 feet (more than seven miles high).

For speed the record may be held by the Peregrine Falcon. J. A. Baker, who developed a kind of love affair with Peregrines and followed them all day every day, described this bird as 'that restless brilliance . . . , that cloud-biting anchor shape, that crossbow flinging through the sky'.[1] He calculated that its ordinary flight speed was between 30 and 40 mph, that in level pursuit of its prey this rose to 50-60 mph, but that when it 'stoops', closing its wings and dropping onto its prey, it reaches 'well over a hundred mph' (p. 21) – while other observers believe this should be doubled.

As an example of persistence or tenacity, I choose the Wandering Albatross, the largest flying bird in the world. At home in the open ocean, even the most ferocious storm conditions do not disturb it. It stays airborne by facing into the wind. Because of a special mechanism which locks its wings open, it can glide for weeks at a time and conserve energy by not needing to beat its wings. It even sleeps on

Right: A Wandering
Albatross riding a
storm in the dreaded
Drake Passage, South
Atlantic.

Right: A Wandering Albatross riding a storm in the dreaded Drake Passage, South Atlantic.

the wing, and comes to land only to breed on some remote Antarctic island.

In chronicling James Cook's return home in *Resolution* in 1774, after his second voyage which circumnavigated the South Pole, Alan Moorehead describes the albatross near Cape Horn:

> *It was always there, each morning at first light, moving up to the ship
> and wheeling around it without so much as a flicker of its immense
> 14-foot wings, a lovely thing, the perfection of effortless motion.
> No distance wearied it; no storm deterred it; when the gale became
> too fierce, it took shelter with outspread wings in the hollows of the
> waves.*[2]

But 'nobility' is the word I have reserved for the Bald Eagle, America's national bird. It was on 20 June 1782, six years after the Declaration of Independence, that Congress voted to adopt the Bald Eagle as the national symbol of America. Not everybody agreed with their decision, however. For example, Benjamin Franklin wrote in a letter to his daughter Sarah Bache on 26 January 1784:

> *For my own part, I wish the Bald Eagle had not been chosen as the
> representative of our country; he is a bird of bad moral character; he*

Above: The East African Fish Eagle belongs to the same genus as the American Bald Eagle. Both are fish-eaters.

does not get his living honestly; you may have seen him perched on some dead tree, . . . too lazy to fish for himself, . . . Besides, he is a rank coward . . . In truth, the Turkey is a much more respectable bird, and withal a true original native of America.[3]

But Franklin was a bit harsh in his judgment. Bald Eagles are as respectable as any predator can be. True, they are scavengers, and pirates too, harassing Ospreys until they give up the fish they have caught. But they exhibit a certain culinary refinement in that their preferred diet is salmon! If we consider other characteristics of the Bald Eagle, we may rather accept the opinion of America's greatest artist–naturalist, John James Audubon. It was on the Upper Mississippi River in 1814 that he first observed the bird and immediately named it 'The Bird of Washington':

As it is indisputably the noblest bird of its genus that has yet been discovered in the United States, I trust I shall be allowed to honor it with the name of one yet nobler, who was the savior of his country . . . He was brave, so is the Eagle; . . . and his fame, extending from pole to pole, resembles the majestic soarings of the mightiest of the feathered tribe.[4]

So, when Ronald Reagan proclaimed 1982 'The Bicentennial Year of the American Bald Eagle', he justified it as follows: 'Its grace and power in flight, its vigilance and loyalty in defending its family group, and most of all its courage, make the eagle a proud and appropriate symbol for the United States.'

No one can deny that the Bald Eagle is a very handsome bird. Of course it is not literally 'bald', but derives its name from the white feathers of its head. Its tail is white too, and its two white extremities, especially when gleaming in the sun, stand out against the dark brown of its body. If one succeeds in getting close, one can also see its bright yellow eyes, beak and feet. It belongs to a family of eight known as the 'Sea Eagles', which include the Fish Eagles of Africa: their haunting call is one of the most authentic sounds of the African bush. One of my experiences of earthly bliss was swimming in Lake Malawi with a pair of Fish Eagles soaring overhead calling to one another.

The very concept of human flight has been inspired by the observation of bird flight, and specially of the flight of eagles. On 8 September 1863 the *New York Herald* announced 'the success of the most extraordinary invention of the age, if not the most so of any the world ever saw'. It was that the medical doctor and inventor Solomon Andrews, Mayor of Perth Amboy in New Jersey, had built and flown a dirigible airship. Andrews called it 'Aereon' 'to symbolise the beginning of a new age'.[5] He was the son of a Presbyterian minister. One Sunday, aged 17, 'he looked out of a church window during his father's sermon and became absorbed by the flight of a Bald Eagle, which was moving through the air without stirring its wings. He felt, he said later, that the simple secret of flight had been shown to him at that moment, and he resolved to place among his numerous ambitions in life the construction of a device that would imitate the eagle.'[6] His second Aereon was airborne in 1866, but he later gave up through lack of funds. Then in 1959, nearly a century later, the Aereon Corporation was formed, in which my friend Bill Miller of Princeton has been heavily involved. Aereon 26, a deltoid-shaped experimental aircraft, had successful manned flight tests in 1971. Since then the US Air Force and Navy have financed further research studies by Aereon.

One of the most successful attempts to dramatise the notion that 'flight is freedom' must surely be *Jonathan Livingston Seagull*, the runaway best-seller by Richard Bach, which was published in 1970. Illustrated by evocative, black–and–white, silhouette photographs of gulls, the most appealing part of the book is its descriptions of flight, which is hardly surprising since its author was a fanatical pilot. We can also applaud Jonathan Seagull's protest against the materialism of other gulls, and his conviction that what mattered most in life was not fishing or fighting but flying, not food but speed (p.54).

But there Christians part company with the message of the book, whose emphasis on self-transcendence anticipated New Age thinking. Jonathan Seagull's ambition knew no bounds. He was determined to fly faster than sound, faster than light, as fast as thought itself. For he knew that 'he was not bone and feather, but a perfect idea of freedom and flight, limited by nothing at all' (p. 63).

Above: A disturbed colony of Kelp Gulls in the South Atlantic.

The application to human beings is easy. We are free, the book implies, to be what we want to be and to go where we want to go, and nothing should stand in the way of our self-actualisation. So when Richard Bach left his wife and his six children, he admitted that freedom was the issue, and that nothing must be allowed to hinder our personal freedom, not even marriage and family.

The biblical road to freedom, however, is the exact opposite. True freedom is not freedom from responsibility to God and others, in order to live for ourselves; it is rather freedom from preoccupation with ourselves, in order to live for God and others. As Jesus himself taught, the way to self-discovery is self-denial. If we insist on living for ourselves, we will lose ourselves; only if we are willing to lose ourselves in loving will we truly find ourselves. Only when we die to our own self-centredness do we begin to live (see, for example, Mark 8:34-37).

Moreover, the biblical symbol of true freedom is not the flight of the seagull but the flight of the eagle. The false gospel of *Jonathan Livingston Seagull* is that 'we can lift ourselves' out of ignorance, materialism and failure (p. 27); the true gospel of Jesus Christ is that *he* is able to lift us. So flight in Scripture is not a symbol of self-effort but of salvation. The picture it presents is not the strenuous flapping of wings, but the spreading of wings to catch the wind, and effortless soaring into the sky.

There are two notable references to the flight of eagles in the Wisdom literature of the Old Testament, both of which emphasize its mystery and majesty. 'Does the eagle soar at your command', God asks Job, 'and build his nest on high?' (Job 39:27). The expected answer is plain. The flight of eagles is beyond human understanding and control. So one of Israel's wise men confessed that, of four things which were 'too amazing' for him, one was 'the way of an eagle in the sky' (Proverbs 30:18,19).

Nevertheless, in spite of the enigmatic nature of eagle flight, it remains a visual emblem of strength. It illustrates the saving power of God displayed in the experience of both the nation and the individual. In describing his rescue of the Israelites from their Egyptian bondage, God said he had carried them 'on eagles' wings' and brought them to

himself (Exodus 19:4). And when even his own people are conscious of their weakness, they can have no higher aspiration than to 'soar on wings like eagles' (Isaiah 40:31; compare Psalm 103:5). This does not represent self-effort, however. For the only people who 'renew their strength', who walk and run without growing tired and who even fly like eagles, are those who wait patiently for the Lord, and put their trust in him (Isaiah 40:29–31).

C. H. Spurgeon, the nineteenth-century Baptist preacher in London, expressed this challenge to faith with his customary eloquence in an address to ordained ministers and ministerial students:

> *Brother, your failure, if you fail, will begin in your faith. The air says to the eagle, 'Trust me; spread thy broad wings; I will bear thee up to the sun. Only trust me. Take thy foot from off yon rock which thou canst feel beneath thee. Get away from it, and be buoyed up by the unseen element.' My brethren, eaglets of heaven, mount aloft, for God invites you. Mount! You have but to trust him.*[7]

1 J. A. Baker, *The Peregrine* (Collins, 1967), p. 12.

2 Alan Moorehead, *The Fatal Impact, the Invasion of the South Pacific 1767-1840* (Hamilton, 1966), p. 187.

3 *The Complete Works of Benjamin Franklin.* Compiled and Edited by John Bigelow, Vol. VIII (London: G. P. Putnam's Sons, 1888).

4 J. J. Audubon, *Ornithological Biography*, Vol. I, 1840-4 edition (Volair Books, New York 1979), p. 55.

5 John McPhee, *The Deltoid Pumpkin Seed* (*New Yorker* 1973; Ballantine Books, 1976) pp. 79-80.

6 Ibid., p. 80.

7 C. H. Spurgeon, *An All-Round Ministry, a Collection of Addresses to Ministers and Students* (1900; Banner of Truth Trust, 1960), p. 29.

Antarctica

Antarctica is the planet's last uninhabited, unspoilt wilderness, although several nations maintain a toehold somewhere on the ice. But so far the continent and its surrounding seas belong to the wild creatures who manage to survive – for example the birds. The albatrosses and petrels arouse our admiration by their powers of flight and of endurance, whereas, according to Dr. Samuel Johnson, the Penguins 'cannot but excite our risibility by their resemblance to human beings'.

Below: A group of Magellanic Penguins coming ashore.

Above: Portrait of a Gentoo Penguin.

Above: The reptilian look of a Tiger Seal, the Penguins' chief enemy.

Below: A King Penguin chick.

Below: The author fraternizing with King Penguins, South Georgia.

8. THE TERRITORY OF ROBINS:
Space

Above: An English Robin flies from its nesting box.

It is characteristic of human beings that we have complementary social and individual needs. On the one hand, as God said in the beginning, it is not good for us to be alone (Genesis 2:18), and commentators have always recognised that this truth has a wider reference than to marriage. We are social creatures by nature. We need each other. We long for authentic relationships. Too much solitude is not good for us. It violates our created constitution.

Yet on the other hand, God has created each of us a unique person, with a unique personality and a unique potentiality, so that he wants us to become ever more fully ourselves. It is unhealthy to lose our individuality in the crowd.

Perhaps in the modern world, especially in the impersonal life of the city, the commoner and the more dangerous of the two tendencies is to forget and even forfeit ourselves. We travel to and from work in crowded trains, and hardly speak to anybody. We are immersed in our responsibilities in the office all day, and in the evening we even allow television to suck us out of the realities of family life into its own fantasy culture. We need to affirm our individuality, to break free from the subcultures which threaten to destroy us, to protest against the loss of privacy, and to make time to be ourselves.

'I need space,' we sometimes say. 'Please don't invade my personal space.' This necessity begins in babyhood. Dr. Donald Winnicott, an acknowledged authority in the development of babies and young children, wrote in his book *Playing and Reality* (first published in 1971) about 'the space between the baby and the mother'. 'From a state of being merged in with the mother, the baby is at a stage of separating out the mother from the self . . .' (p. 107). Later Dr. Winnicott expresses this essential separation or breakaway in violent terms as 'a life-and-death struggle' (p. 145), since the child cannot become an adult without it.

The demand for personal space, however, is particularly a symptom of adolescence, when we emerge out of childish dependence on our parents into a necessary independence. So teenagers often defend their territory against intruders. They post a notice on the outside of their bedroom door, which says 'Private. Keep out. Entry by invitation only.' Thus, while not rejecting membership of the family or of the wider world, the adolescent is asserting the adult's right to privacy, to space.

And what 'space' is to humans, 'territory' is to birds. The fundamental part played by territory in the bird's annual cycle of courtship, mating, incubation and parenthood has only recently been discovered. The ground-breaking book on this topic was written by H. Eliot Howard, entitled *Territory in Bird Life*, and published by Murray in 1920. There are some very interesting parallels between birds and humans in the establishment and assertion of territory.

Below: An American Robin at Yellowknife, Canada. The American Robin (*Turdus migratorius*) is not a robin at all, but a thrush.

Let's take as our main example of territorial defence the robin. Ah, but which robin? North Americans who visit Europe, and Europeans who visit North America, soon discover that both continents have a 'robin'; and most visitors probably assume that they are one and

the same transatlantic species. Certainly both are popular songbirds, inhabit gardens and woodland, develop a familiar relationship with human beings, have a sweet warbling or whistling song, enjoy a diet of earth worms and insects, have a tendency to fly south in the winter, and sport a dramatic red breast.

But there the similarities end. The American Robin (*Turdus migratorius*) is actually not a robin at all, but a thrush! It got its familiar name from early British settlers who, remembering the 'Robin Redbreast' of their home country, jumped to the conclusion that the redbreasted American thrush was a robin too. It is so popular in the United States that three states have chosen it as their bird, namely Connecticut, Michigan and Wisconsin.

The European Robin (*Erithacus rubecula*) is an altogether different species. If anything, it is even more popular than its distant American cousin. For it is Britain's national bird, and it appears every year on millions of Christmas cards. It is smaller than a sparrow, its legs are thinner than match sticks, and it is remarkably tame and confiding. It also has the distinction of being the first bird to have had its biography written. For it is the subject of a learned monograph, entitled *The Life of the Robin* by David Lack,[1] who in 1945 became director of the Edward Grey Institute of Field Ornithology in Oxford. It is a

Below: The European Robin (*Erithacus rubecula*), Britain's national bird.

Right: Robins are fierce in defence of their territory.

Below: Charles Haddon Spurgeon, the late nineteenth-century prince of Baptist preachers.

rigorous, scientific, though popular investigation into the life history and habits of the robin.

Many people have given the robin an undeserved reputation for piety. For example, after the death of Charles Haddon Spurgeon, the prince of Baptist preachers, in 1892, large numbers gathered in Norwood Cemetery, South London, for the funeral. 'As the service proceeded,' one of Spurgeon's biographers has written, 'a little robin poured forth its liquid note . . . from a neighbouring tombstone. The redbreast made appropriate music, fabled as it was to have had its crimson coat ever since it picked a thorn from the Saviour's bleeding brow.'[2]

David Lack discovered, however, that 'the pious bird with the scarlet breast, our little English robin' (Wordsworth) is extremely pugnacious. After its annual moult in July and August, from the beginning of September the cock robin establishes his territory. Then his sweet melodious song is intended neither to express his own pleasure, nor to bring pleasure to his mate. No, 'the most important use of song to the robin in its territory is to advertise possession to rivals and to warn them off' (p.36). 'In the early spring the song also serves to advertise the unmated cock in possession of a territory to hens in search of mates' (p. 38). When David Lack introduced a stuffed robin into the territory of a pair of living robins, they first postured,

Above: A colony of Common Guillemots (or Murres) on Skokholm Island, off Pembrokeshire, West Wales. Guillemots and razorbills occupy communal ledges, laying their single egg on the bare rock.

Below: A colony of dainty, caterwauling kittiwakes.

giving a menacing display of their red breast, and then attacked the dead bird so violently as on one occasion to decapitate it and on another to demolish it altogether.

Robins spend so much time and energy establishing and defending their territory, that we naturally become curious about the purpose of this procedure. What is the value of territory to birds? Scientists are still debating this question, but there seems to be a degree of consensus. Territory (1) facilitates the acquisition and retention of a mate, (2) guarantees an adequate food supply for the young, (3) disperses the population, spacing them out in the suitable habitat available, and (4) prevents other pairs from interrupting the raising of several broods.

Bird territories vary greatly in size from about an acre (in the case of most smaller perching birds) to as much as thirty square miles (in the case of the large eagles). But in each situation the birds vigorously defend their territory, maintain its invisible boundaries, and chase off interlopers.

Further, even colonial nesters are still territorial. I think of the seabird colonies I know so well on 'The Wick', a perpendicular cliff-face on Skomer Island in south-west Wales. On its upper reaches the fulmars nest; the middle area is occupied by both razorbills and guillemots (Murres); and below them, not far above sea level,

Above: A colony of King Penguins in their 'rookery' on South Georgia, in the South Atlantic.

is a colony of dainty, caterwauling kittiwakes. The fulmars and the kittiwakes at least have their own nest sites to defend. The guillemots and razorbills, however, occupy communal ledges, laying their single egg on the bare rock. Yet each pair still guards its own minuscule egg-space. And if an individual bird needs to trespass into another's space, it walks past in a stylised mincing gait in order to assure the rest of the colony that its purposes are entirely innocent.

Or I think of the huge number of King Penguins which lay their single egg in their 'rookeries' on South Georgia in the South Atlantic, and of the 30,000 pairs of gannets which build their nests on Grassholm, another island off the coast of West Wales. In both cases the sitting birds, the penguins and the gannets, look like a well laid-out orchard, as each is just beyond pecking distance from its neighbour.

Thus these seabirds are both colonial and territorial at the same time. And so are many modern city-dwellers. Our high-rise apartment blocks somewhat resemble the perpendicular sea cliffs; the thousands who occupy the apartments somewhat resemble the densely populated seabird colonies; and as these close colonies enjoy a measure of protection against predators, so the large numbers of apartment block residents offer them a measure of mutual security. Both situations

Right: The huge gannet colony on Grassholm, an island off the coast of West Wales. Each bird is just beyond pecking distance from its neighbour.

combine the colonial (massed numbers) and the territorial (individual space to be defended).

Christians are anxious to preserve this combination of colony and territory, and to avoid extremes. Although the ratio between the two varies from culture to culture, authentic human existence must include both; for either without the other would be destructive of our created humanness.

On the one hand, to surrender to the pressures of mass culture, to have no privacy, no time for reflection on the fundamental issues of life, and no opportunity to grow into the unique person God has made each of us, is to lose a vital part of ourselves.

On the other hand, as solitary confinement is regarded as a peculiarly cruel punishment, so to live a hermit's life is to deny both our creation as social beings and our Christian calling into *koinonia* (fellowship). The eastern mystic looks forward to ultimate absorption into the Divine, as a droplet of water is absorbed into the ocean. But Christians know that God's purpose for us is not to lose but to retain our created individuality. The Christian life begins when Christ stands at the door of our heart and knocks (Revelation 3:20). He will not invade our space. Only when we open the door to admit him will he come in.

1 1941; Pelican, 1953.
2 Quoted by Lewis A. Drummond in *Spurgeon Prince of Preachers* (Kregel, 1992), p.755.

9. THE WINGS OF A HEN:
Shelter

One of Jesus' most direct allusions to bird life was to a hen, meaning the female chicken of the farm yard, which 'gathers her chicks under her wings' (Matthew 23:27). He chose this familiar sight as a picture of God's love, and in particular of the shelter from judgment and disaster which his love provides. In using this metaphor, he was drawing on a long Old Testament tradition, which spoke of finding refuge under the 'shadow' or 'shelter' of God's 'wings'.

Everybody knows that birds are warm-blooded vertebrates, and that essential to the definition of a bird is its covering of feathers and its possession of wings. Its feathers help to regulate its body temperature, protecting it from sudden, drastic climate changes. Consequently, every feather is important and has to be kept trim, and all birds spend time each day in preening operations, passing their bill

Right: Jesus alluded to a hen, which 'gathers her chicks under her wings' (Matthew 23:27), choosing this familiar sight as a picture of God's sheltering love.

Above: Ostriches at Amboseli, Kenya. The ostrich, the largest bird in the world, uses its diminutive wings to gain momentum and for display.

along every feather (often appearing to 'nibble' it), in order to get rid of unwelcome parasites, to clean and smooth the barbs so that they lock into one another, and to distribute water-resistant oil from the preen gland which is located near the base of the tail.

Even the small number of birds which cannot fly use their wings for other kinds of propulsion. An ostrich, for example, which is the largest bird in the world and can weigh up to 200 kg. (more than 30 stones), yet uses its diminutive wings to gain momentum and for display. Xenophon, the fourth century BC Greek general and historian, had observed this. He wrote: 'An ostrich no one succeeded in catching; those horsemen who hunted that bird soon desisted from the pursuit; for it far outstripped them in its flight, using its feet for running, and its wings, raising them like a sail.'[1] Xenophon was correct. Horses can gallop at 40 mph, but ostriches when chased can reach 50 mph. As God commented to Job, 'the wings of the ostrich flap joyfully', even though 'they cannot compare with the pinions and feathers of the stork', or indeed of other flying birds (Job 39:13).

The most agile flightless birds are the penguins. They literally fly under water, using their wings and tail to twist and turn with extraordinary agility, either when chasing a fish or when being chased by their chief enemy in Antarctic waters, the Tiger Seal.

The nearest equivalents to penguins in northern waters are the auks, especially the puffins, razorbills and guillemots. One of the most enjoyable sights each summer, for those of us who have access to the North Atlantic, is of that comic clown the puffin which somehow manages to chase and catch, and then clasp side by side in its massive and colourful beak, half a dozen or so sand eels. Speaking of fishing birds, which use their wings to swim under water, honourable mention should also be made of the cormorants, which can often be seen standing on a rock with wings spread out to dry in the sun.

Apart from underwater swimming, birds use their wings for at least six other purposes. The first is balancing. Normally birds can stand steadily on any perch. But if the foothold itself becomes unstable, and especially if the wind gets up, a delicate balancing act becomes necessary, for which the bird's wings offer a marvellous versatility.

The second and third uses of a bird's wings both relate to the

Above: Two squatting puffins near The Wick, Skomer Island, West Wales.

approach of an intruder. Some species, especially the plovers, are adept at feigning injury, dragging a wing along the ground as if it were broken, at the same time crying most piteously, in order to distract the interloper and entice him away from the eggs or the young. Others adopt a fearsome aggressive posture and, if this fails, boldly attack the enemy, inflicting either a hefty whack with the wing (e.g. swans and geese) or a sharp jab with the spur (e.g. Spur-wing Plovers), neither of which the intruder is likely to forget.

Fourthly, some birds use their wings in the act of fishing or hunting; for example, the African Black Heron, which I have watched on the edge of Lake Naivasha in Kenya. Wading in the shallows, and stalking with slow stealth, as all herons do, the Black Heron regularly unfolds and raises both wings to form a circular umbrella or hood. The purpose of this so-called 'canopy feeding' is either to attract fish into apparent shelter or to render them more visible by reducing the sun's glare.

The fifth use of wings is in courtship display, which in some cases is elaborate and beautiful. For example, the polygamous Australian Lyrebird runs to its display mound in the forest (see p. 88), raising and fanning out its wings and tail, 'padding' with its feet, and uttering strange guttural noises.

In other species, while the female remains on her nest, the male displays by sound rather than by sight. Male snipe, for example, fly high above the tree tops, then turn earthwards in a steep dive, holding their fluttering wings in a fixed position, and causing bleating, buzzing or drumming sounds (according to their species) as the air rushes through their extended tail feathers. In yet other species both sexes use their wings in mating display. Swans and grebes face each other on the water, standing tall and raising their wings, while albatrosses and cranes face each other on land and use their wings to the fullest advantage in an uninhibited nuptial dance.

But a bird's sixth use of its wings, which is also frequently alluded to throughout the Bible, is in the protection of its eggs and its chicks. Nearly all birds incubate, sitting on their eggs in order to keep them warm. Moreover, once egg-laying is complete and incubation has begun, most parents show a marked reluctance to leave the nest.

Above: The rare Ross's Goose – with its gosling at Lake Karak, in the uninhabited Canadian Arctic.

Some rely on camouflage to escape detection and sit motionless. An Eider Duck will sit tight until an intruder actually touches her. Such devotion is the more remarkable when the nest has no natural cover and is exposed to the elements. For then the sitting bird is the only available protection either from the merciless heat of the tropical sun or from the bitter cold of an Arctic or Antarctic blizzard.

Once the eggs have hatched, almost nothing will induce the mother bird to abandon her chicks. I recall visiting an island on Lake Karak in the uninhabited Canadian Arctic, on which both Snow Geese and the much rarer Ross's Geese were nesting. In a rusty old tin can, which had been hidden in a cairn at one end of the island, a message informed us that this breeding ground of the geese had been discovered eight years previously. My friends and I were distressed, however, that as we waded ashore from our Cessna on floats, and gingerly approached the sitting geese, they all got up from their nest and walked away. All except one, that is, and as we stalked it, we suddenly saw why it did not move. Peeping out from under one of her wings was a gorgeous golden gosling! In fact, the chicks of many ground-nesting birds leave the nest within a day or two of hatching, and then the mother has a repertoire of clucks and calls, which warn them of an enemy's approach and tell them either to freeze or to come running to her for shelter.

The very first allusion to birds in the Bible (even though an oblique one) occurs in its second verse, where the Holy Spirit, in his creative role in relation to the primeval chaos, is described as 'hovering over the waters' (Genesis 1:2). In another Old Testament verse the same Hebrew verb's reference to birds is explicit. In Deuteronomy God is said to have 'shielded . . . and cared for' his people 'like an eagle that . . . hovers over its young' (Deuteronomy 32:10f.). And later, when the inhabitants of Jerusalem were threatened with an Assyrian invasion in the eighth century BC, the prophet Isaiah promised that, if they put their trust in God, he would protect them: 'Like birds hovering overhead, the LORD Almighty will shield Jerusalem; he will shield it and deliver it, he will "pass over" it and will rescue it' (Isaiah 31:5). It is remarkable that God's promise to shield Jerusalem against enemy attack in Hezekiah's day reminded Isaiah not only of a mother bird protecting her young,

Above: A Blue Goose (a dark phase of the Snow Goose) and gosling at Lake Karak, Canada. Once her eggs have hatched, almost nothing will induce the mother bird to abandon her chicks.

Below: A Rough-legged Hawk feeding its young chicks in their nest; near Sachs Harbour, western Arctic.

but also of the first Passover when God 'passed over' Israelite homes to protect them from his own judgment (Exodus 12:23).

So the conviction that a bird will 'care for her young under the shadow of her wings' (Isaiah 34:15) became a readily recognizable metaphor of God's loving care and protection of his people. 'The shadow of his wings' passed into the language more as a symbol to be interpreted than as a picture to be visualized. (The literal notion that God has feathers is a bit grotesque!). It occurs at least six times in some of the great psalms of personal devotion. First, it comes as a statement of joyful confidence: 'Because you are my help, I sing in the shadow of your wings' (Psalm 63:7). Next, it expresses an aspiration ('I long to . . . take refuge in the shelter of your wings', Psalm 61:4), a determination ('I will take refuge in the shadow of your wings', Psalm 57:1) and a prayer ('Hide me in the shadow of your wings', Psalm 17:8). But it is more than a statement of individual commitment; for God's steadfast love binds him to all the people of his covenant, whatever their social status may be: 'How priceless is your unfailing love! Both high and low among men find refuge in the shadow of your wings' (Psalm 36:7). Indeed, anybody and everybody who makes God his trust will experience his protection, for 'he will cover you with his feathers, and under his wings you will find refuge' (Psalm 91:1, 4).

Above: A view of Jerusalem from the Mount of Olives. It was here that Jesus appealed to Jerusalem: *'O Jerusalem, Jerusalem . . . how often I have longed to gather your children together, as a hen gathers her chicks under her wings, but you were not willing!'* (Matthew 23:37).

That this promise extended beyond God's covenant people and embraced even aliens, is made clear in the beautiful story of Ruth the Moabitess. Famine had driven Elimelech from Bethlehem to Moab, together with his wife Naomi and their two sons Mahlon and Kilion. The sons later married Moabite women, Orpah and Ruth. In due course all three men died, leaving Naomi and her two daughters-in-law without male protection. Having heard that the famine in Judah was over, the three widows prepared to return there. Naomi did her utmost to persuade her daughters-in-law to leave her and go back to their own Moabite family, and after many tears and kisses Orpah did so, 'but Ruth clung to her' (Ruth 1:14). With courage and determination she declared: 'Where you go I will go, and where you stay I will stay. Your people will be my people and your God my God' (Ruth 1:16).

The Book of Ruth goes on to tell how in God's good providence she met and married one of Naomi's relatives called Boaz, and how their son Obed became David's grandfather. For our purposes, however, we need to note what Boaz said after he had learned of her love and loyalty in leaving her family and homeland and joining the people of Judah. 'May you be richly rewarded by the LORD, the God of Israel', he said, 'under whose wings you have come to take refuge' (Ruth 2:12).

What, then, did Jesus have in mind when he appealed to Jerusalem and used the analogy of a mother bird? 'O Jerusalem, Jerusalem,' he cried, 'you who kill the prophets and stone those sent to you, how often I have longed to gather your children together, as a hen gathers her chicks under her wings, but you were not willing!' (Matthew 23:37 = Luke 13:34). Jerusalem had had a long history of rebelling against God's word. Often God had longed to welcome his people and spare them his just judgment, if only they would come back to him in penitence. But they kept rejecting his grace. Now Jesus identified himself with God in issuing a final appeal. But it was too late. Today's world also needs deliverance from many disasters – economic collapse, environmental degradation, socio-political violence and nuclear war. But none is greater than the just judgment of God on those who reject his gospel.

The imagery of the hen gathering her chicks into safety under

Above: A colony of nesting Spoonbills on a Hungarian lake.

her wings is a touching picture of God's grace. And as Jesus used it, he was clearly and deliberately developing a feminine image of God. He found in the Old Testament ample precedent for doing so. For there God promised that he would comfort Israel 'as a mother comforts her child' (Isaiah 66:13). He also insisted that his love is even greater than a mother's love, since she may forget her baby, whereas he would never forget his people (Isaiah 49:15). Moreover, in a daring verse in the Song of Moses he describes God as both father and mother to Israel. For he is 'the Rock who fathered you' and 'the God who gave you birth' (Deuteronomy 32:18). Although this does not give us liberty to address God as 'our mother', since he invariably reveals himself as 'our father', and Jesus told us to approach him thus, nevertheless it obliges us to remember that our Father-God has motherly qualities. To this great truth we are also directed by the picture of the mother hen with her chicks.

1 Xenophon, Vol. I *Anabasis* 1.v.3. Tr. J. S. Watson (George Bell, 1907), p. 21.

Penguins

There are fifteen different species of penguins in the world, mostly concentrated in the seas surrounding Antarctic ice. Though flightless, they can 'fly' underwater at more than 25 mph.

Overall: The author engaged in some precarious cliff-ledge photography.

Top far left: Two King Penguins in a courtship 'beaking' display.

Left: Adelie Penguins are real Antarctic birds, entirely at home in those glacial waters.

Below far left: A pair of Rockhopper Penguins, which can jump up an almost perpendicular cliff.

Below left: A Chinstrap Penguin stands watch over her two chicks.

10. THE SONG OF LARKS
Joy

Above: A wren opens its throat to sing, balancing lightly on grass.

Hail to thee, blithe spirit!
Bird thou never wert,
That from heaven, or near it,
Pourest thy full heart
In profuse strains of unpremeditated art!

(Percy Bysshe Shelley, *Ode to a Skylark*, 1819)

Birds and humans have obvious characteristics which distinguish them from one another. Birds can fly; humans cannot. Humans can make moral choices; birds cannot. Yet they have at least one thing in common: both sing! Both have vocal chords, even though ours is the larynx and theirs the syrinx.

Moreover, each bird species has its own distinctive song by which it can be recognised. Two rather nondescript little greenish-yellow warblers – the Chiffchaff and the Willow Warbler – were originally thought to be the same species. They both nest in Europe and winter in Africa, and their look-alike plumage can deceive even experts. But Gilbert White, the Hampshire parson and author of *The Natural History of Selborne* (1789), insisted that they must be distinct species because of their distinct songs. The former goes 'chiff-chaff-chaff-chiff' in a harsh, irregular and even erratic fashion, whereas the Willow Warbler utters a sweet cadence in a descending scale, in a minor key, and with a final flourish.

A good friend of mine, Dr. David Howard, formerly general secretary of the World Evangelical Fellowship, and now President of the Latin America Mission, has told me how during his boyhood his father, a keen naturalist, had learned to imitate bird calls. He was able even to assign a particular call to each member of the family. David's

Above: A skylark sings on the ground, at Llantysilio Mountain, North Wales.

mother was the Chickadee, his brother Philip the Meadow Lark, his sister Elisabeth the Wood Peewee, and he himself the Tufted Titmouse. He recalls how one day, when he was walking down Broad Street, Philadelphia, in the noise of the noonday traffic, his father saw him half a block away and whistled to him. He spun round instantly, his ear having become attuned to the call of the Tufted Titmouse.[1]

Only the tone-deaf could fail to appreciate the liquid bubbling trill of the curlew's spring song, the haunting yodel of the Great Northern Diver (Common Loon in North America), the resonant, explosive outburst of the wren ('Winter Wren' in North America), its tiny throat palpitating like a prima donna's, the melodious flute-like warbling of the male European Blackbird, or the Song Sparrow's varied repertoire of up to twenty-five little arias.

Of special mention is the so-called 'dawn chorus', in which all the local breeding birds join in, heralding the sunrise. Viscount Grey, whom I have mentioned in an earlier chapter, used to escape from his parliamentary duties in London to Fallodon, his estate in north-east Northumberland. Though towards the end of his life his eyesight was failing, his hearing remained keen, and he loved the summer dawn chorus, which was at its best between three and four o'clock

Above: A European Goldfinch. Goldfinches and linnets continue to give voice in captivity, though it is now against the law in many countries to cage wild birds.

in the morning. 'Unfortunately', he wrote, 'this wonderful opening of the day occurs at an hour when civilised man is either in sleep or suffering from the want of it. In the first case he does not hear the singing; in the second he is in no mood to enjoy it; is, in fact, not worthy of it.'[2]

It is a grievous expression of human depravity that, whenever something good has been discovered, somebody is ready to market it. So even song birds have been caged and turned into merchandise. Luckily, skylarks sing only when free and fall silent in a cage. Nightingales too seem to need their freedom if they are to do justice to the full-throated music of their song. But African Canaries continue to give voice in captivity, and so do some of the finches like goldfinches and linnets. I should have said 'did' not 'do', for it is now against the law in many countries to cage birds. In Britain, for example, The Wildlife and Countryside Act 1981 gives birds full protection. Although it is still legal to breed many species in captivity, it is an offence to take and/or keep a wild bird.

The Romantic poets were not slow to celebrate our principal songsters. Both John Keats and William Wordsworth followed John Milton in composing an *Ode to a Nightingale*, whereas Wordsworth and Shelley both wrote an *Ode to a Skylark*.

The Eurasian Skylark is somewhat drab in appearance, but compensates by its sensational song. Although a ground-dwelling and ground-nesting bird, its real habitat is the sky. In song flight the male ascends vertically, higher and higher, until it is almost out of sight. As it hovers, head to wind, with vigorous wing beat, its song is delivered with enormous gusto. Its high-pitched, shrill, forceful warbling is sustained for up to five minutes, with apparently no pause for breath, until it parachutes down, with a final, silent drop to the ground.

Poets less well-known than Wordsworth and Shelley have also tried to capture the lark's unique combination of flight and song. I think of Mary Sorrell, who came to Christ in later life, following a stroke which deprived her of speech. It was then, when her vessel was floundering and near to sinking, that (she wrote) 'I found Jesus Christ treading the blue-green waves' (p.13). Here is her poem about the lark:

Overall: A skylark singing in flight.

In a grey sky,
  On a grey day,
A brown lark sang
  Her roundelay.

With trembling voice
  And quiv'ring wing,
She hovered low
  To softly sing.

No sweeter song
  I ever heard
Than from the throat
  Of that small bird.

She trilled and trilled,
  Then flew away,
Into the sky
  And sunless day.[3]

From the merchants and the poets we come to the scientists who delve into the meaning of bird song. Not that they are able to explain the songs of birds in purely functional, reductionist terms. Even

Right: When one is walking across a European marsh, a Redshank is often the first bird to sound the alarm with its high-pitched, haunting, melodious call.

Above: In most North American marshes, from the Atlantic to the Pacific, male Red-winged Blackbirds can be seen displaying their scarlet epaulettes. Their calls vary from a liquid gurgle to a plaintive whistle.

when resolved to cultivate objectivity and eschew sentimentality, they cannot help conceding that birds sing for the joy of it, and for the necessary release of emotional energy.

The variety of their noises is phenomenal. They whistle and warble, trill, twitter and tweet, chirp, croak, quack and cackle, coo and crow, squeak and squawk, scream and shriek, wail and whine, hoot, honk, boom and pipe. Human language is not rich enough to express all the sounds they make. It is usual to distinguish between their 'songs' and their 'calls'. Yet both are standardised signals which have been interpreted and classified in different ways. Dr. W. H. Thorpe of Cambridge University, an acknowledged expert in animal behaviour and bird 'language', divided bird calls into ten groups. Perhaps it is legitimate to simplify this list a little and suggest six main functional bird calls.

(1) Birds call to advertise their presence, so as to attract a mate and/or assert their territory.

(2) Birds call to warn of danger from a predator.

(3) Birds call to threaten a rival or intruder.

(4) Birds call to keep contact with each other when they are passing through a forest or migrating.

(5) Birds call to accompany nuptial display and invite mating.

(6) Birds call to reassure their chicks in the nest and to rally them when they have left it.

Human speech is of course a much more sophisticated medium of communication than the wordless songs and calls of birds. Yet there are similarities between singing humans and singing birds. To begin with, the main outburst of avian song takes place in the breeding season and is associated with courtship and mating. Just so, some of the greatest human songs have always been love-songs, variations on Romeo serenading Juliet. We also resort to national anthems and patriotic songs, to express our solidarity with each other, and to pop music to encapsulate our sense of cultural identity. *Joie de vivre* also demands musical expression. On occasions of congratulation and

Above: The congregation of All Souls Church, Langham Place, London, are led in praise by choir and orchestra. The most appropriate of all occasions for singing is the public worship of Almighty God.

celebration it is natural to break into singing 'Happy birthday to you', 'For he's a jolly good fellow' or 'Auld lang syne'.

But the most appropriate of all occasions for singing is the public worship of Almighty God. Many people do not know how special – even unique – singing is to Christians. Temples, synagogues and mosques never resound with the exuberant praise of those who know their sins have been forgiven. The joyful song of the redeemed is heard only in Christian churches, and never with greater exultation than in Charles Wesley's hymns like 'And can it be?', 'Love divine, all loves excelling', 'Hark! the herald angels sing' and 'O for a thousand tongues to sing'.

There was of course singing in the temple worship of Old Testament days, and the Psalter is full of invitations to praise God:

> *Come, let us sing for joy to the LORD;*
> *let us shout aloud to the Rock of our salvation.*
> *Let us come before him with thanksgiving*
> *and extol him in music and song.*
> (Psalm 95:1, 2)

Above: The inevitable consequence of being filled with the Spirit is that we sing 'psalms, hymns and spiritual songs' (Ephesians 5:18,19).

Sing to the LORD a new song;
sing to the LORD, all the earth.
Sing to the LORD, praise his name;
proclaim his salvation day after day.

(Psalm 96:1, 2)

It is also taken for granted in the New Testament letters that the singing of hymns will be a natural and spontaneous expression of Christian praise. The inevitable consequence of being filled with the Spirit, and of having the word of Christ dwell richly within us, is that we sing 'psalms, hymns and spiritual songs', making music with gratitude in our hearts to God (Ephesians 5:18, 19; Colossians 3:16). Christian people are irrepressible in this matter. It would be impossible to stop us singing.

Further, the Book of Revelation assures us that the angels, the created universe and the completed church will finally unite in singing a new song of praise to God, affirming the unique worthiness of the Lamb to open the book of destiny and to receive all honour, glory and praise (Revelation 5). In particular, the redeemed people of God, from every nation, tribe, people and language, standing before God's throne, will cry out in a loud voice:

Salvation belongs to our God,
who sits on the throne,
and to the Lamb.

(Revelation 7:9, 10)

The church has always recognised that the three highest peaks of the mountain-range of salvation are the incarnation, the atonement and the resurrection. So it is that the greatest hymnody of the church has focused on these three events and their significance. For example, 'Once in royal David's city' celebrates the incarnation, 'There is a green hill' the atonement, and 'Jesus Christ is risen today' the resurrection.

It is here that we part company most decisively with the birds. Perched on some conspicuous twig, with beak lifted high and throat

vibrating violently, a bird will seem to sing its head off. Scripture even says, metaphorically speaking, that it is engaged with all nature in worship:

> *Praise the LORD from the earth, . . . wild animals and all cattle, small creatures and flying birds . . . Let them praise the name of the LORD.*
>
> (Psalm 148:7, 10, 13).

But of course this is a pure anthropomorphism. Singing birds have no idea what they are doing. And we must not copy them in this. Bishop John Jewel of Salisbury saw this clearly in his *Second Book of Homilies* (1571). In the homily entitled 'Of Common Prayer and Sacraments' he wrote that we must sing 'with the reason of man, not with the chattering of birds'. To be sure, he continued, 'ousels and popinjays and ravens and pies and other such like birds are taught by men to prate they know not what; but to sing with understanding is given by God's holy will to the nature of man'.

We cannot sing with joy and gratitude to the Lord unless we sing with understanding.

1 From a personal communication to the author on 12 February 1977.
2 Viscount Grey of Fallodon, *The Charm of Birds* (Hodder, 1927), pp. 87–88.
3 Mary Sorrell wrote her story in *Out of Silence* (Hodder & Stoughton, 1969).

Flamingoes

Overall picture: The majority in this flock are Lesser Flamingoes. The Greater Flamingoes are those standing tall.

The soda lakes of Kenya's Great Rift Valley are the breeding and feeding grounds of huge numbers of flamingoes. When they assemble in a flock of 2-3 million, turning the shoreline of a whole lake pink, especially Lake Nakuru, one is witnessing one of the best ornithological spectacles in the world.

Flamingoes engage in 'filter-feeding'. That is, they sweep their head and neck from side to side in shallow water. They then use their tongue to pump out the water they have taken in, while some 10,000 platelets in their mouth retain the microscopic algae, and a few small animals as well.

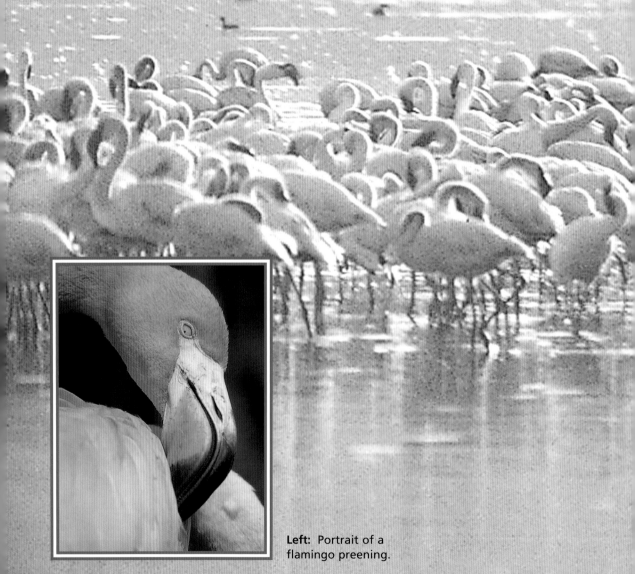

Left: Portrait of a flamingo preening.

Above: In flight flamingoes stretch out their head, neck and legs to the fullest possible extent.

Above: Flamingoes at Lake Nakuru, Kenya.

Right: A flamingo engaged in filter-feeding.

11. THE BREEDING CYCLE OF ALL BIRDS
Love

Above: A breeding colony of kittiwakes in Eire.

Everybody knows that love is the greatest thing in the world. No human experience excels love. Love has inspired the finest art and the noblest heroism in the history of the world. Living is loving, and without love the human personality disintegrates and dies. Moreover, Christians know why love is supreme. It is because God is love in his innermost being (1 John 4:8, 16), and because, when he made us in his own image and likeness, he gave us too the capacity to love. No wonder Jesus coupled two Old Testament verses, one from Deuteronomy and the other from Leviticus, and declared that to love God and to love our neighbour are the first two of all the commandments, adding that 'there is no commandment greater than these' (Mark 12:28-31). Then Paul went on to affirm that love is eternal and will never cease (1 Corinthians 13), while John taught that its pre-eminent expression has been in Christ and his cross. For 'this is how we know what love is,' he wrote: 'Jesus Christ laid down his life for us' (1 John 3:16).

Now love implies relationships (it cannot exist without them), although relationships do not necessarily imply love. We need to be cautious, therefore, when we are investigating sub-human relationships. It is understandable that we should indulge in 'anthropomorphisms', speaking of animals as if they were humans, and attributing to birds sentiments and actions which belong to human beings alone. But it is a tendency we should resist. For, although virtually all creatures engage in activities which resemble ours, we have no liberty to assume, for example, that 'courting, mating and parenting' mean the same to birds as they do to humans. Similarly, although birds have the most developed family life of all vertebrates except mammals, 'family' to humans means something different in kind and quality from what it means to birds.

Above: A small family of Cattle Egrets has colonized this tree near Madurai, in South India.

Many birds are gregarious by nature, as is evident from the collective nouns which are used in relation to them. We have probably all heard of a covey of partridges, a bevy of quails, a paddling of ducks, a spring of teal, a gaggle of geese and a herd of swans. Less well-known, however, are a charm of goldfinches, a murmuration of starlings and an exaltation of larks.

First, some birds feed together. A notable example is the communal fishing of Great White Pelicans. Up to a dozen birds swim in a horseshoe formation, with the open end pointing forward. Then from time to time, in perfect unison, as if in response to a signal, they all plunge their heads into the water and bring up whatever fish they have enclosed.

Secondly, many birds congregate for night-time roosting, to protect themselves from predators and from the winter cold. As the sun dips down towards the horizon, small flocks fly in from all directions towards their favoured rendezvous. I have myself watched extraordinary gatherings of hornbills in a Thailand forest, Scarlet Ibises collecting on mangrove trees in Trinidad's Coroni Swamp, and egrets in Africa and Asia alighting on a given tree until it is white with these elegant herons. No roost is more spectacular, however, than that of European Starlings, which turn the sky black as more than a million

Above: A Magnificent Frigatebird on North Seymour Island, Galapagos. Males in the breeding season develop a bright crimson throat pouch, which they inflate like a balloon and exhibit to passing females.

Below: An Australian Lyrebird in display.

may fly in, to gather on trees or city buildings.

Thirdly, some birds breed colonially, as was mentioned earlier, and fourthly, most birds which migrate do so in flocks. Geese, swans and duck fly in V-formation, so as to avoid the slipstream of the bird in front, and so conserve energy. Raptors use thermal currents and so drift in large but irregular numbers. Perhaps the most extraordinary mass migration is that of Australian 'mutton birds', the popular name for the Short-tailed Shearwaters. Millions of them migrate in a huge loop around the Pacific, from South Australia to Japan and back again.

The breeding cycle of all birds, prompted by hormonal changes, is in three main stages. The first is courtship and mating, the second nest-building, egg-laying and incubation, and the third parenting. There is a wide variety of behaviour in all three. Woody Allen's half-serious, half-humorous quip in his film *Manhattan* was 'I think people should mate for life, like pigeons or Catholics.' He is quite right that some birds are monogamous and form a pair bond which lasts until it is broken by death. Swans and geese belong to this category. But the duration of the pair bond varies considerably, and the majority of birds find a new mate every year.

To attract a partner the male displays his distinctive plumage to its greatest possible advantage. One extraordinary example is the Magnificent Frigatebird, which breeds on tropical oceanic islands. Males in the breeding season develop a bright crimson throat pouch or gular sac, which they inflate like a balloon and exhibit to passing females, adding noise to colour by vibrating their bodies and rattling their bills.

Other birds are polygamous, not least those males which make use of a communal 'lek' or display area, to which they attract several admiring females. These include the Eurasian Black Grouse and the Ruff, several species of North American Grouse, and most notably the spectacular Birds of Paradise of Papua New Guinea. Their display combines pantomime, ballet and opera. They not only spread their wings and their tail feathers, in order to exhibit their colourful plumage, but they simultaneously dance and sing, and in one case even hang upside down. This exotic male display is usually followed by mating with several females.

Right: A Red (or in Europe 'Grey') Phalarope at Cambridge Bay. In all three of the world's Phalaropes sexual roles are reversed. The brighter colouring belongs to the female, the duller to the male, who also incubates the eggs and feeds the chicks.

So the courtship ritual is almost always performed by the male, who shows off his colourful, often iridescent plumage, in order to impress and win one or more females. A surprising exception concerns the three species of phalaropes, sometimes referred to as 'swimming sandpipers', which breed in the far north. In their case the sexual roles are reversed. The brighter colouring belongs to the female, the duller to the male, who also incubates the eggs and feeds the chicks.

The elaborate courtship ritual of other birds includes flight – soaring, parachuting, swooping, rolling or diving. The hummingbirds seem to delight in daring stunts. But their acrobatics are not the prelude to marital fidelity. 'Each male is a feathered Don Juan,' writes Crawford Greenewalt, 'with interests limited to food, fighting, and courtship . . . Hummingbirds are largely polygamous and promiscuous' (p. 22).

Nest-building is the beginning of the second stage of breeding. Some birds are content with a simple, little scraping on the ground. Others occupy a convenient hole in a bank, tree or building. Bald Eagles return to the same nest every year and add to its bulk until it may be twenty feet deep and weigh more than a ton. Weaver-birds and Tailor-birds are well named, as the most intricate sewing goes into the making of their nests. Orioles build hanging structures. Swallows

Above: White Storks greeting each other near Lake Manyas, Turkey.

restrict themselves to mud. Others employ sticks, reeds, seaweed, leaves, and dry grass. They then bond it with tree resin, spider or caterpillar silk, or (in the case of swifts) their own saliva. Next, they line it with feathers, animal fur, plant fibre, moss or lichen. And finally some birds decorate their nest with anomalous bits and pieces like string, paper and rag.

Once the nest has been built and the eggs have been laid, the seemingly tedious period of incubation begins. In the case of small birds it lasts only about ten days, but three months elapse before the Wandering Albatross's egg hatches. Concentration is required too, because the eggs need to be regularly turned so that every surface comes into contact with the parent's 'brood patch', an area of bare skin and superficial blood vessels which supplies warmth. Gannets instead place one of their webbed feet on the egg to keep it warm. Even more remarkable is the procedure of the Australian 'megapodes' or mound builders (e.g. the Mallee Fowl and the Brush Turkey). The male first digs a pit and then scrapes together a huge mound of decaying vegetation like a compost heap, topped with sand, and uses his tongue to test the heat, which he keeps at exactly 92°F. All the female does is to lay her eggs in the pit which serves as an incubator. When the young hatch, it takes them several hours to burrow their way out of the mound. From that point onwards they are entirely independent. They feed themselves and fly, and have no contact with either parent.

In other cases, after the chicks have hatched, their parents continue to keep them warm and feed them assiduously. Roger Tory Peterson has mentioned a pair of Great Tits which made 900 visits to their nest in one day. That this is an obsessional, undiscriminating instinct, and not comparable to the loving care of human parents, is evident. For it continues unabated even when the rightful chicks have been forcibly ejected by an intruder, a social parasite like a Eurasian Cuckoo or a North American Cowbird.

We sometimes talk about the parental care, devotion and self-sacrifice of birds. But no, in spite of obvious similarities, avian pair-bonding is not monogamous marriage; the attention of parents to their young from hatching to independence is not self-sacrifice; and the technique of bird copulation is not to be compared to the

Right: A Common Redstart carrying food to its young; Rasa, Switzerland.

'one flesh' experience which God has instituted to symbolise and enrich the loving union of two human personalities in matrimony (Genesis 2:24).

Human love is unique, because it is a reflection (pale perhaps but authentic) of the eternal, selfless love of God himself, revealed on the cross, affirming the worth of its human objects, and leading to the 'steadfast love' of his covenant pledge to his people. So far from elevating bird behaviour by the use of extravagant anthropomorphic language, we should feel rebuked when they appear superficially to outshine us. The real mystery is not that birds can behave like humans, but that humans can behave like God.

Below: The Alaskan Brown Bear, backlit by the morning sun, scavenging along the edge of a lake.

Below: Two male King Eider Ducks near Cambridge Bay.

Below: The Arctic Ground Squirrel, which the Inuit call 'Siksik'.

Below: An Arctic Wolf, at Polar Bear Pass, Bathurst Island, Canada.

Below: A majestic Musk Ox.

Arctic Birds and their Habitat

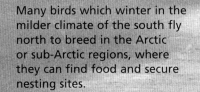

Many birds which winter in the milder climate of the south fly north to breed in the Arctic or sub-Arctic regions, where they can find food and secure nesting sites.

Overall: The cluster of buildings known as Bathurst Inlet Lodge at the mouth of the Burnside River.

Below: A Lesser Yellowlegs perched precariously on the topmost twig of a spruce tree, near Churchill, Manitoba.

Below: A male Rock Ptarmigan in winter plumage.

Below: A Red-throated Loon (or 'Diver') near its Arctic nest.

Conclusion

Psalm 103 and Psalm 104 make a significant pair. Both are invitations to worship. And both begin and end with the same formula: 'Praise the LORD, O my soul'. But Psalm 103 celebrates the goodness of God in salvation, forgiving our sins and keeping his covenant, whereas Psalm 104 celebrates the greatness of God in creation, establishing heaven, earth and sea, and sustaining their creatures with life and food.

In his rehearsal of wildlife in Psalm 104 the psalmist twice makes an honourable mention of 'the birds of the air'. He refers to their main activities, singing and nesting, and relates them to the Lord's well-watered trees:

> ¹² *The birds of the air nest by the waters; they sing among the branches. . .*
> ¹⁷ *There* [that is, in the trees] *the birds make their nests; the stork has its home in the pine trees.*

Here, then, is an early allusion to ecology, that is, to living creatures in their natural environment. God both plants and waters the trees; the birds both sing and nest in them. Indeed, all creatures are dependent on their environment, and loss of habitat is the major cause of loss of species.

It was Jeremiah in the seventh century BC who foretold the evils of habitat destruction. He combined the roles of patriot and prophet, and it caused him great anguish. He was torn between his patriotic love for his own country and his prophetic warning of God's coming judgment on it. If the people stubbornly maintained their refusal to repent, he cried, the Babylonian army would invade from the north

Right: A Wandering Albatross with its 12-foot wingspan on its nest on Prion Island, Antarctica. Let us do all we can to protect and preserve our unique God-given environment, and enjoy its 'biodiversity', not least its birds.

and would devastate the land. Four times he repeated his statement 'I looked.' He looked at the earth and the heavens, at the mountains and the hills, at city and sky, at orchard and town, and each time he saw only destruction. The earth had again become 'formless and empty', having returned to the primeval chaos of Genesis 1:2; the heavens had become dark, as they were before God had said 'let there be light' (Genesis 1:3); the mountains were quaking and the hills swaying. Worst of all, there were no people, and there were no birds, for 'every bird in the sky had flown away'. Why? Because 'the fruitful land was a desert' and 'all its towns lay in ruins before the LORD, before his fierce anger'.[1]

We would do well to reflect on Jeremiah's warning of a possible return to pre-creation chaos, darkness and devastation. One of God's creation blessings was the appearance of birds to 'fly above the earth across the expanse of the sky' (Genesis 1:20); one of his judgments would be their disappearance.

So let's resolve to do all we can to protect and preserve our unique God-given environment, and so continue to enjoy its God-given 'biodiversity', not least its fascinating birds.

In Britain we are proud of the Royal Society for the Protection of Birds, which recently celebrated its centenary and now has more than a million members. It owns and manages about 120 Reserves.

Nobody seems to know how the avocet came to be the symbol

Above : An avocet approaches its nest; Gyldenstern, Denmark. The avocet is the symbol of the Royal Society for the Protection of Birds.

of the RSPB, but it is certainly appropriate. For avocets disappeared as a breeding species in the UK in the middle of the nineteenth century, and reappeared only in 1947 in Suffolk, when one group nested at Minsmere, and another on Havergate Island. Thanks to the energetic activities of local birdwatchers, and to the extraordinary measures taken by the RSPB at Minsmere to create a habitat suitable for avocets, they are once again well-established breeding birds.

In the United States the National Audubon Society, named after the nineteenth-century American naturalist and artist, John James Audubon, was founded in 1905 and has more than 200 local 'chapters'. Dedicated to conservation of all kinds, it wages an unremitting war against such evils as air pollution, pesticides and deforestation.

Much smaller and more recent, but increasingly international, is the organisation called A Rocha, which is sub-titled 'Christians in Conservation'. Founded in 1983 by Peter and Miranda Harris, who are now its international co-ordinators, it is an innovative combination of Christian witness and care for God's creation. Its first field centre was set up in the Algarve (Portugal); the story is told by Peter Harris in his book, *Under the Bright Wings* (Hodder & Stoughton, 1993). Initiatives are now being taken to establish similar centres in Lebanon, France, Kenya, Argentina, Britain and Poland.

Peter Harris was kind enough to read this book in manuscript, and so has saved me from several ornithological howlers. I am very grateful.

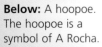

Below: A hoopoe. The hoopoe is a symbol of A Rocha.

1 Jeremiah 4:23-26. The tragic disappearance of 'the birds of the air' as a result of divine judgment is a regular theme of the prophets. See Jeremiah. 9:10 and 12:4; Hosea 4:3 and Zephaniah 1:3.

Addresses
The Royal Society for the Protection of Birds, The Lodge, Sandy, Bedfordshire, SG19 2DL, UK
The A Rocha Trust, 3 Hooper Street, Cambridge, CB1 2NZ, UK
The National Audubon Society, 700 Broadway, New York, N.Y. 10003, USA